D1170549

EQUAL CIRCLES
Women and Men in the Bahá'í Community

EQUAL CIRCLES

Women and Men in the Bahá'í Community

Edited by Peggy Caton

Kalimát Press
Los Angeles

First Edition

Copyright © 1987 by Kalimát Press
All Rights Reserved

Manufactured in the United States of America

"Recovering a Lost Horizon:
Women's Contributions to North
American Bahá'í History"
Copyright © 1987 by Jackson Armstrong-Ingram

Library of Congress Cataloging in Publication Data

Equal circles: women and men in the Bahá'í community.
Contents: Religion and the myth of male superiority/
Baharieh Rouhani Ma'ani—Recovering a lost horizon/R.
Jackson Armstrong-Ingram—Two career couples/Judy Maddox
—[etc.]
1. Women, Bahá'í. 2. Women in the Bahá'í Faith.
3. Equality—Religious Aspects—Bahá'í Faith. 4. Sexism—
Religious Aspects—Bahá'í Faith. I. Caton, Peggy.
BP370.E68   1987   297'.89178343   87–21373
ISBN 0–933770–60–X

Kalimát Press
1600 Sawtelle Boulevard
Suite 34
Los Angeles, California 90025
(213) 479–5668

To
CORINNE TRUE
for her great service to the cause of
women and her pioneering efforts to
promote equality in the Bahá'í community

CONTENTS

Introduction

THE MEN WERE THE ACTIVE ONES in our Bahá'í study class, proving and challenging. The class was clearly a male arena, although the men didn't see it that way. A core group of men chose the topics, arguing and challenging each other in free academic debate. Although they might notice that women didn't participate fully, they took this as a sign that they were either disinterested or incapable of rigorous intellectual discipline. The need for evidence and linear logic was taken for granted in this group. Without these tools, women—and men for that matter—were not taken seriously. Feelings and impressions had to be backed up with "facts" to be acknowledged at all. If someone got hurt in the fray, it was because he didn't know how to play the game, or she couldn't stand up under close scrutiny.

The core group of men were those who worked in an office together, and their network of male friends. They had established this group as a testing ground for new ideas in Bahá'í scholarship and often tried to outdo each other in challenging convention. They soon developed in their discussions an easy style of bantering and joking, dismissing those who lagged behind or who didn't share their knowledge. The women, of course, had relationships with these men and competed for the most powerful among them.

In a rather vague way I didn't like what was going on. I wasn't really interested in the scholarly focus—but I knew any opposition would be smashed and taken as a sign of incipient conservatism. This was the place to be among intellectuals, and I wanted to be counted. I pretty much kept out of the action, however, watching what others were doing, content and not content to sit on the sidelines. As time passed, I felt less and less inclined to enter the discussions. Anyone who did so risked being verbally destroyed.

At one session of our long-standing class, without plan or warning, the women individually and simultaneously challenged the format. Many of us had been sitting there quietly for years, listening to male speakers and presenters expound on topics important to them. Both the topics of discussion and the nature of the discussion itself had finally become unacceptable to us. This unexpected protest divided our class, and the division was along gender lines.

I don't remember at all what the class was about that day, just the usual crowd debating Bahá'í topics. Nor do I recall exactly what caused our reaction. Maybe it was the continued orchestration of events by the core male group, or perhaps one woman's futile attempt to make a divergent point, or the finality of the intellectuals' victory over their challengers.

After the class, the women gravitated toward each other to express their insecurities, their discomfort, and dissatisfaction with the class. We discovered that most of us felt the same way. At that moment, we no longer felt alone and isolated. Feelings long denied welled up into an explosion as we gathered with the men to reveal our discovery—that something was wrong with the study class. We dredged up feelings of powerlessness, lack of voice in the class, and exclusion from the old boy network running it.

The men there were Bahá'ís, and most considered themselves feminists. Some thought themselves to be much more so, in fact, than the beleaguered women who were so angrily protesting. They were bewildered and angered by this attack, coming out of nowhere—there had been no inkling of unrest up to this point. They insisted that the women's objections had nothing to do with gender. It was natural, they said, that in any group some are more dominant than others, according to ability. They told us that we weren't saying anything that made sense, that we were going around in circles, and offering no evidence. It was hard, if not impossible, to give the men the specific evidence they demanded. They could only respond to our feelings and impressions with frustration and anger, concluding we had nothing substantial to say—only hollow, erroneous accusations. The men were not discriminating against women, nor was that even an issue, they asserted. Everyone had equal chance to speak. And then, perhaps, we didn't feel it was a gender issue either. We just happened to be a group of women protesting.

At every opportunity the men dismissed sex and equality as an issue. But not always in a direct or conscious manner. They would ignore points, demand evidence acceptable to them and then dismiss it as trivial, or produce examples of men and women who didn't fit the pattern. They would respond in an intimidating manner, giving curt answers, or raising their voices in outrage while firing off a barrage of questions, exceptions, and demands for proof:

"Men dominate the discussion here and create a hostile atmosphere."

"Women can participate if they want. If you don't like it, change it. Give me one example of hostility."

"Your tone of voice right now is one."

"You're too sensitive. We've always allowed everyone equal time."

We were in a "one-down position" trying to get the men to accept our arguments, to accept the validity of what we were saying, and to change. All they had to say was: "No, I don't accept," or "No, I won't change," and they had us.

In the free-for-all of that day, it became apparent that there was division and difference in thinking—the bewildered men retreating in their sense of betrayal, and the angry women releasing infuriated feelings of discrimination and oppression. It seemed that even among this highly educated, liberal group of Bahá'ís, the equality of men and women still existed only in name.

The women were challenged by the men of the class to make a study group presentation. But we never did so. We felt that if we gave this presentation, unless we could make an air-tight case, we would be subject to the humiliation of having our arguments torn apart. And we would risk having this issue dismissed for all time. Without the presentation, the men would feel triumphant: "Well, we gave them their chance, and they weren't up to it." Many of the issues weren't clear to us women, either. We needed time to reflect and present our findings in a format where we would not be interrupted by immediate and hostile rebuttal.

At the same time, these issues were important to more than just the members of our study class. Some of the women decided to make our presentation in the form of this collection of essays. We would explore issues that hurt, puzzled, and angered us. We would attempt to reach out to other women, to explain ourselves to men, and to clarify and explore issues of gender identity and equality.

As the essays developed, however, and new women who were not part of the class contributed their ideas, our focus changed. We realized that equality is not just a woman's issue, it is an issue that demands the attention of both men and women. Beyond equality loom major issues of gender identity, translating ideals into practice, and overcoming millennia of male dominance. It is not simply a matter of making women identical to men. Nor is equality just proclaiming that different functions are equal (any more than separate but equal spelled equality for blacks during segregation). And it is certainly more than: "Oh, yes, equality. We have always believed in that."

Bahá'u'lláh, the Prophet and Founder of the Bahá'í Faith, proclaimed the equality of men and women as one of His most important principles, giving it no less an exalted position than that of an essential prerequisite to world peace. The Bahá'í Writings discuss the necessity of education, opportunity, and encouragement for women; the gradual unfolding of her potential; and the necessity of attaining balance and equity between the sexes. The progress of civilization and the attainment of a unified and just social order are to be founded on equality—between men and women and among peoples and nations.

Believing in these ideals, then, perhaps one day while perusing the *Kitáb-i Aqdas* (Bahá'u'lláh's Book of Laws) a Bahá'í may notice—but not mention to anyone—that the Bahá'í inheritance laws consign a greater share of wealth and property to male relatives of the deceased than to the female relatives.[1]

One gradually realizes that in addition to the Writings that stress equality, there are those that stress differences between men and women: the primacy of motherhood, exclusion of women from the military and from the Universal House of Justice (the highest administrative institution of the Faith), uneven distribution of inheritance, dissimilarities of temperament and spiritual capacity.

Trying to integrate all these admonitions into personal and community life a Bahá'í must face two challenges: (1) adjusting previous attitudes and practices of inequality to fit a new ideal; and, (2) reconciling dilemmas posed by the seeming contradictions found within the Bahá'í Writings themselves. This struggle is reflected in all of the essays.

The essays by Ma'ani and Armstrong-Ingram discuss women's role in the history of the Bahá'í Faith, illustrating discrepancies between doctrine and practice, illuminating previously omitted contributions of women, and explaining the gradual evolution of equality of practice within the Bahá'í community. Maddox's article grapples with the issue that every Bahá'í woman, especially, must face when she reads the Writings: how to reconcile the emphasis found there on motherhood with the emphasis that is also placed on women's achievement in science, art, and politics.

Next, Jaspar explores the psychological consequences of oppression to women who have been conditioned from infancy to feel "less than." Bradley portrays the grim reality many women face when their sense of identity and self-worth depends on being loved by a man. The essay on gender relations treats traditional expressions of masculinity and femininity as two very different cultures which together result in suppression of the feminine.

Gender identity itself has become confused in the quest for equality. Rice and Morrison explore the painful consequences of failing to conform to traditional female and male roles. Haithman's essay on the black experience provides an alternative perspective on women's concerns. For example, black American women have always had to work outside the home. Therefore, they consider irrelevant the dilemma of whether a woman should work or stay at home with children. Finally, when it comes to raising children, Armstrong reminds us of the complexities of the struggle to translate ideals into practical realities.

In integrating the Bahá'í Texts into their lives, Bahá'ís, as individuals and as communities, face the dilemma of whether to understand these Writings in an absolute sense, or in a relative sense: historically, culturally, or individually. For example, the statement ". . . the world of women should be a spiritual world, not a political one, so that it will be radiant,"[2] made by 'Abdu'l-Bahá, the eldest son and successor of the Bahá'í Prophet, could be taken as absolutely and literally true for all times and all places. This presents a problem, however, when one tries to reconcile it with His statement: "So it will come to pass that when women participate fully and equally in the affairs of the world, when they enter confidently and capably the great arena of laws and politics, war will cease . . ."[3]

Understanding the first statement in historical context, as addressed to early Bahá'í women in Iran, helps us see it as part of a gradual development of women's position within the Faith. But it does raise the new question of how and whether to apply this admonition to our own time and place.

Each Bahá'í community will perceive and act on this question influenced by its own traditions and tendencies. The above quotations can certainly be understood differently in different cultural settings. However, since inequality is an integral part of gender roles in almost all societies, cultural relativity too is problematic. A number of the essays in this book point out the discrepancy this traditionally ingrained inequality has produced between the intent of religious injunctions and how they are carried out.

The Bahá'í Faith originated in the Middle East at a time when women's status in society was often on a par with that of the household furnishings. As Armstrong-Ingram points out, early Iranian Bahá'í men brought to the United States the understanding that women were not eligible for service on local Houses of Justice. And, as both Armstrong-Ingram and Ma'ani point out, important women's contributions to the development of the Faith have simply been omitted from Bahá'í history—certainly a statement about values and the power of unstated assumptions in determining what is important.

Concepts of "spiritual" or "essential" equality can be abstractly applied to conditions of the greatest practical inequality without any seeming contradiction to those who do so. For example, many Bahá'ís view women and men as simply having different functions: women in the home raising children, and men in the workplace producing goods and services. They proclaim these separate spheres as fully equal, even when as a result women end up serving tea and taking minutes at Bahá'í committee meetings due to inexperience in public decision-making processes and lack of opportunity to develop their leadership potential. The argument might then continue: that serving food and taking notes is "spiritually" equal to holding positions of leadership, making decisions, and affecting public policy.

When I was in Iran, during the 1970s, there was much talk among Bahá'ís of different but equal spheres. The result was that, at the National Convention in Tehran one year, I could count only two women delegates out of more than one hundred representatives. Were the rest at home taking care of children? Equality is more than a label to be applied to traditional patterns of inequality, formerly justified by society on other grounds. It must be reflected in real social conditions. On some spiritual level, yes, the cleaning lady is equal to the bank president. But is she fully equal? Does she have equal choices, opportunities, status, and freedom? Does she have equal opportunity to become bank president?

During the last decade in the United States, many came to believe that equality meant sameness. As Rice points out, in actuality this sameness meant that women were expected to become like men, to discard their "identities of oppression" in order to adopt "equal" careers and behaviors. Women put on their suits and took their briefcases into the corporations to compete with their male counterparts for power, status, and position. Only then could they earn the right to equality (which was, of course, judged by the standards of the men who ran those same corporations). The traditional women's roles of nurturance were devalued and avoided by both women and men—leaving the care of children, for example, to paid professionals (usually women) many of whom were themselves from oppressed groups within society.

Seeing in this male-oriented androgyny a further devaluing of women, perhaps as damaging as the traditional "different but equal" response, many feminists argued for the feminization of social institutions and of the men that ran them. The Bahá'í Writings themselves point to this need for balancing the qualities of masculine and feminine:

> . . . *the new age will be an age less masculine, and more permeated with the feminine ideals—or, to speak more exactly, will be an age in which the masculine and feminine elements of civilizations will be more evenly balanced.*[4]

In addition to our culturally determined understanding, we have the problem of individual application. We may believe that many of the Bahá'í Texts were written for individual circumstances and are really applicable only to those to whom they were written. But then the question of applying these Writings to our personal lives becomes even more baffling.

In response to these puzzles, some Bahá'ís retreat into black-and-white thinking, trying uniformly to reconcile all differences, hoping to find definite answers that will apply to every circumstance. Failing to do so, they may finally throw up their hands and say, "It's up to the individual."

But the Bahá'í Faith, while extolling the role and value of the individual, is not an individualistic religion. Bahá'ís are creating social institutions and a social context as parameters for individual and group development. Local Spiritual Assemblies act as creators of community, governed by general principles and rules of interaction. Individuals act within networks of relations which center around a structure of such calendar events as Bahá'í Feasts and Holy Days. Within this structure, Bahá'ís meet, marry, divorce, raise children, and develop a community life based on the enactment of Bahá'í principles—universal education, the elimination of prejudice, and the establishment of a system of laws that regulates and establishes standards for an entire world community.

The individual, then, exists within society; and thus the issues of sexual identity and equality cannot be resolved in isolation. We live in societies where male standards dominate and define the social system. These standards are reflected in social institutions, economic processes, and political ideologies. Intertwined in the struggle for equality and definition is the clash of values and ideologies which envelop and influence interpersonal relations. Although change on the personal or interpersonal level can affect society without changing social institutions and their values as well, gender and family relations become fragmented, disrupted, and disunified.

In our struggle towards equality, therefore, the purely personal response cannot ultimately provide the answer. Nor can a uniform centralized response. Only the creation of flexible norms that allow for individual variation and creativity can meet the challenge presented by such a worldwide and heterogeneous community as the Bahá'í Faith offers. With the equality of men and women seen as a flexible norm, the exact behavior of men and women in regards to staying home with children, for example, or working outside the home, is not rigidly specified. But the necessity of ensuring balance and fairness is. As Shoghi Effendi, Guardian of the Bahá'í Faith from 1921 to 1957, explains: "There are, therefore, times when a wife should defer to her husband, and times when a husband should defer to his wife, but neither should ever unjustly dominate the other."[5]

Although either husband or wife may stay at home, or work outside the home, the equity of the arrangement must be the guiding principle. Husbands often expect their working wives to do all or most of the housework and child-rearing in addition to their employment outside the home, because motherhood is her "role." Is that equitable? Or, a traditional homemaker may expect her husband to take over all the household and child care duties when he is not at his job, so that she can pursue her individual development. Is that equitable?

The male standard has long been accepted as the psychological and social standard of human behavior. This has affected our view of Bahá'í history as well as our concept of equality. And, indeed, it was one of the issues reflected in our study class struggles. The ubiquity of the male standard emerges as the hidden agenda in equality issues. It is not spoken of directly—it is assumed. These assumptions are reflected in subtleties of interpersonal relations and communication styles, in situational discrimination, and in hierarchies of dominance and submission.

The confining nature of traditional male and female roles and behavioral norms has oppressed many spirits, leaving women particularly with a sense of inferiority, powerlessness, and loss. One of the dilemmas in defining the female identity is deciding whether old and established women's values and behaviors are the undesirable results of oppression, or are merely different and valuable, or are both. If they are merely different, why don't women have equal status, power, and privileges? Why, for example, in our study class, weren't women presenting topics or contributing equally to the discussion?

Among themselves women encourage an equal sharing of ideas and feelings. Women's style of speech tends to be other-supportive, while that of men is self-assertive. In a mixed-sex group, therefore, it is the men who generally define the topics, determine and lead the discussion, and carry the momentum of the projects. Both men and women have valuable insights and perspectives to contribute to a group discussion. Since the nature and topics of conversation for women often differ from those of men, this imbalance in contributing, with men leading and women following, prevents both from benefiting from the dynamic process of discussion that would occur if they could pursue a dialogue on an equal basis.

The question of equality has almost always been addressed by Bahá'ís as a woman's issue. It has thus been seen as a woman's task, almost exclusively, to make herself equal to man. The insights of this book show that both men and women must become equal. If there is imbalance, particularly in power and privilege, adjustments must be made on both sides. This is not an easy task, as most men will not willingly give up their power; indeed, in many cases they are unaware of just how their dominance manifests itself. In most cases, then, it will inevitably be women who first create awareness of inequity and who advance the practice of equality in the community by demanding equal rights, privileges, and respect. All Bahá'ís—both men and women—need to adhere to the words of Bahá'u'lláh that teach that they have been created worthy and are equally beloved in His sight.

The Bahá'í community must go beyond words and rhetoric: we must examine our behavior and attitudes and ask if they truly reflect the equality we so confidently proclaim we have. Too often we have settled for premature answers, for stereotypes of both gender identity and equality. Instead of regarding the subject as closed and settled, our further development requires us to keep an open mind, to regard equality as a process, one that will always call for questioning, probing, and seeking new understandings.

Equal Circles: Women and Men in the Bahá'í Community is the third in a series of books relating social issues to the Bahá'í teachings. The first two volumes in the series are *Circle of Unity: Bahá'í Approaches To Current Social Issues* and *Circle of Peace: Reflections on the Bahá'í Teachings.* The essays in this book represent another step toward understanding and realizing equality in our lives. They reflect many points of view, and some may disagree with others. Each piece represents only the view of the individual author, and none pretends to offer an official Bahá'í position. The essays here do not exhaust the gender issues currently debated in society. They are intended to inspire discussion and encourage further work, both on these issues and on others not represented here. We are grateful to all those who have helped and supported us in our work over the last few years and to the men and women of the study class whose long-remembered discussion launched the essays in this book.

PEGGY CATON
LOS ANGELES

Notes

1. *A Synopsis and Codification of The Kitáb-i-Aqdas* (Haifa: Bahá'í World Centre, 1973) pp. 43–44.
2. *Women: Extracts from the Writings of Bahá'u'lláh, 'Abdu'l-Bahá, Shoghi Effendi and the Universal House of Justice* (Ontario: Bahá'í Canada Publications, 1986) p. 6.
3. Ibid., p. 42.
4. Ibid., p. 13.
5. Ibid., p. 32.

EQUAL CIRCLES
Women and Men in the Bahá'í Community

Religion and the Myth of Male Superiority

by Baharieh Rouhani Ma'ani

FROM TIME IMMEMORIAL, men have assumed superiority over women. Man has used every available means to develop his own capacities and abilities—powers that God had bestowed equally upon the male and female members of the human race—but prevented woman, through the introduction of arbitrary rules, from availing herself of the same rights, privileges, and opportunities. Though many religious teachings of the past sought to raise the status of women, these were often lost, discarded, or reinterpreted by men in their effort to degrade women's position.

With the Revelation of Bahá'u'lláh, a new age was proclaimed. Bahá'u'lláh revealed the principle of the equality of the sexes and established it as a prerequisite for the attainment of the unity of humankind, the very purpose of His mission. 'Abdu'l-Bahá after Him affirmed the central importance of this teaching to all believers and expounded on the necessity of eradicating all forms of prejudice and inequity against women.

The Origins of Male Domination. There has been much speculation about the origins of the inequality of men and women in society. As 'Abdu'l-Bahá asked:

3

Neither sex is superior to the other in the sight of God. Why then should one sex assert the inferiority of the other, withholding just rights and privileges as though God had given His authority for such a course of action?[1]

The male's abundance of physical strength gave him the illusion that his was a superior sex. This notion of male superiority no doubt started from home and family—and later extended to the greater family, to society, community, nation, and world. Man's past ignorance blinded him to the realization of the true spiritual equality of men and women. He vainly imagined that since he excelled in physical force, this was the proof of his perfection. He could not see past the physical realm. Woman's lofty attributes of compassion, tenderheartedness, selfless love, sacrificing nature, and her need for protection and material sustenance to carry out the function of procreation were interpreted as signs of weakness and exploited to the fullest.

Such physical criteria of superiority did not take into account woman's gift of intuition. Man did not appreciate her more developed sensitivity to the need for nurturance, receptivity, and human reciprocity. The very virtues that distinguished women from men and made them loving, caring, motherly human beings, in a world governed by material values, were held up as proofs that women were intrinsically inferior to men.

Since women could not overcome men's physical strength, which became the touchstone of their superiority, they had to accept their inferior position. They satisfied themselves with the nourishment of generations of children whose very survival depended on their selfless and sincere sacrifice. Women paid the cost of saving the world of humanity from men's ambition and destructive arrogance through their extraordinary powers of fortitude and endurance.

The illusion of male superiority, coupled with intense involvement in the affairs of the world, kept men from developing the full and proper use of their own spiritual instincts. They used their assumed authority to decree that women be consigned by nature to a station of suffering and maltreatment. Centuries of repression and inhibition reduced the status of women to lower than human. According to 'Abdu'l-Bahá's testimony:

> *In past ages it was held that woman and man were not equal —that is to say, woman was considered inferior to man, even from the standpoint of her anatomy and creation. She was considered especially inferior in intelligence, and the idea prevailed universally that it was not allowable for her to step into the arena of important affairs. In some countries man went so far as to believe and teach that woman belonged to a sphere lower than human.*[2]

Today we can recognize that the biological differences that were held up as signs of superiority and inferiority simply make each sex fit to undertake the functions that it can best perform. The acceptance of the role that each sex plays in the creative plan of God safeguards the best interests of humanity and ensures the continuity of a well-balanced and functional world. The bestowal of different physical capabilities is for the purpose of producing a unifying whole, mirroring forth the perfections of humankind.

But in the past, the contrary view was taken. And the expression of this view is found in the records of past religions —or so it appears, judging from the texts of the various holy scriptures. A satisfactory answer to the perplexing question of what role religion played in supporting the notion of male superiority is beyond the scope of this paper. It seems doubtful that religion was the origin of these ideas. But there is no question that religion and religious teachings have been used to support and validate theories of male supremacy.

Bahá'ís believe that man's capacity for the comprehension of the truth has evolved over time. Religion has progressively played a primary role in the development of his powers of understanding. In order to turn man to God, to subdue his animalistic tendencies, to attune him to the world of spirituality, and finally to achieve its purpose, religion has had to make allowances for the circumstances of the times. This necessity seems to have demanded accommodation of the practice of the inequality of the sexes, which existed even before the advent of religion.

The Founders of the divine religions sought to bring some kind of law to the unruly and wild primitive man. Religion, therefore, acknowledged his established superiority over women—gained by his physical force—in order to satisfy his thirst for power and authority. It seems that men's grip on the affairs of women was so firm and profound that religion could not affect a sudden change. The requirements of the times and the immaturity of humankind made the pronouncement of the equality of the sexes impracticable and beyond reach.

Therefore, the religions of the past found it necessary to make allowances for men's superiority in order to inculcate in them the need for spirituality. Gradually, religion was able to educate man in spiritual teachings. He was brought to the realization that the true purpose of religious practice is to train humanity to forgo selfish demands and animalistic drives and allow the rule of conscience and truth to reign in its life.

There is abundant evidence that the Founders of past religions introduced provisions into religious law intended to gain a better and more human status for women. But these laws and provisions were exploited and distorted by the very men whom the divine Educators were sent to tame. They misinterpreted the utterances of the Prophets and used them as a pretext to maintain their superior status. The original words of the scriptures lost their intended meaning and purpose. The result was that, although at the beginning of every new revelation commandments were given that improved the status of women, over time their situation gradually deteriorated until it returned to the lowest depth.

The basis of this conjecture is that a study of the passages of written scripture that refer to the status of women will show that they are far more favorable toward women than are the interpretations introduced by others at a later date. While the authentic scriptures might acknowledge a slight difference in the status of men and women, such passages were invariably used centuries later to justify the most brutal injustices inflicted on women—the men maintaining that this was desired by God, and the women accepting the maltreatment, believing that they were indeed created to accept the will of men.

Women in Biblical Teaching. The first chapter of the book of Genesis establishes the equality of men and women, in that they were both created in the image of God and there is no distinction made as to their status:

> So God created man in his own image, in the image of God created he him; male and female he created them. And God blessed them . . .[3]

This initial record of the equality conferred upon men and women is immediately followed in the Old Testament by another account of creation, however. In this account, woman is created from the rib of man. Clearly the purpose of this story was to lower the status of woman to a dependent and subordinate one. Thereafter, the woman is deceived by a serpent and partakes of the fruit of the forbidden tree. The man also eats of the fruit of the same tree, fully aware that he is disobeying the instructions of God. But it is the woman who is made to suffer the severest punishment:

> Unto the woman he said, I will greatly multiply thy sorrow and thy conception; in sorrow thou shalt bring forth children; and thy desire shall be to thy husband, and he shall rule over thee.[4]

The capacity of woman for childbirth is here presented as a curse and punishment. How could divine justice ordain this? This glorious capacity for motherhood is here presented as a proof of woman's inferiority. 'Abdu'l-Bahá has said in this connection:

> *If we take this story in its apparent meaning, according to the interpretation of the masses, it is indeed extraordinary. The intelligence cannot accept it, affirm it, or imagine it; for such arrangements, such details, such speeches and reproaches are far from being those of an intelligent man, how much less of the Divinity . . . [I]f the literal meaning of this story were attributed to a wise man, certainly all would logically deny that this arrangement, this invention, could have emanated from an intelligent being. Therefore, this story of Adam and Eve who ate from the tree, and their expulsion from Paradise, must be thought of simply as a symbol.[5]*

'Abdu'l-Bahá then proceeds to give the new meaning of the story, relieving women of the onus placed upon them from the beginning of history by this ancient tale.

In some Christian teaching, however, this story is presented as God's literal, revealed word, to be accepted and followed without question. It becomes the basis of further and endless assumptions by men, advancing their own cause and depriving women of their religious and human rights.

Other Christian scriptures, in some passages, advocate inequality between the sexes—especially in the epistles of St. Paul. He confirms the superiority of man by introducing him as the head of woman:

> But I would have you know, that the head of every man is Christ; and the head of the woman is the man; and the head of Christ is God.[6]

Other derogatory statements with regard to the status of women can be found:

> Let your women keep silence in the churches: for it is not permitted unto them to speak; but they are commanded to be under obedience, as also saith the law.[7]

And:

> Let the woman learn in silence with all subjection. But I suffer not a woman to teach, nor to usurp authority over the man, but to be in silence. For Adam was first formed, then Eve. And Adam was not deceived, but the woman being deceived was in the transgression. Notwithstanding she shall be saved in childbearing, if they continue in faith and charity and holiness with sobriety.[8]

The use of the veil during prayer or profession is prescribed for women:

> For if the woman be not covered, let her also be shorn: but if it be a shame for a woman to be shorn or shaven, let her be covered. For a man indeed ought not to cover his head, for as much as he is the image and glory of God: but the woman is the glory of the man. For the man is not of the woman; but the woman of the man. Neither was the man created for the woman; but the woman for the man.[9]

Based on Paul's interpretation of the teachings of Jesus Christ, Christian women have failed to this day to achieve an equitable status with men in the orthodox churches.

The Status of Women in Islam. A careful study of Islam, which is closer to us in time than other past religions and which possesses the authentic utterances of its Founder, reveals the extent of the improvements the Prophet Muhammad sought to effect in the status of womanhood. Such improvements, however, eroded gradually as a result of the interpretations of those who considered themselves the exponents of His Holy Book, until they culminated in the tragic plight of women's utter submissiveness to the dictates of men.

The Prophet of Islam was raised as an orphan—first by His mother, Áminih, and later by His foster mother Halímih. As a fifteen-year-old youth, He became the trusted employee of an affluent widow, Khadíjih, who was engaged in trading. She became Muhammad's first wife and His only consort for nearly twenty-five years. Khadíjih played a significant role in Muhammad's life, both at the time when He received the first intimation that He was a prophet, and in the early developments of that religion.

When Muhammad shared with Khadíjih His prophetic experience—which had puzzled and terrified Him—she immediately bowed herself in acceptance of it. She confessed the truth of the Revelation He had received, and she gave Him the encouragement and support necessary to advance the Claim.

The Prophet Muhammad had four daughters born of Khadíjih. They became instrumental in linking the Prophet with very important factions of the Arabian tribes, uniting them through matrimony with each other. Three of the daughters married two of the first four Caliphs who succeeded the Prophet; and one caused her husband, an enemy of Muhammad, to embrace Islam. His youngest daughter, Fátimih, who was joined in wedlock with His favorite cousin 'Alí, the first Imám of Shí'ih Islam, is the most outstanding heroine of that dispensation. She is the link between the Prophet and the Imáms who followed 'Alí.

Muḥammad, after the passing of Khadíjih, married many wives, all of whom came from diversified backgrounds and were widows, except for one or two. These wives of the Prophet provided another means of unity for the warring factions of the people of Arabia, who were drawn closer together by virtue of the link established between them and the family of Muḥammad. There are other important contributions made to Muslim history by the early female believers in Islam which are recorded in the books of that religion.

The favorable influences and the loving attitudes of Khadíjih and other women in the life of Muḥammad as a child, a youth, and a Prophet, may be one of the factors which influenced the elaborate and practical steps He took to improve the degraded status of women in the Arabia of that day. He knew through personal experience that women deserved better treatment. The inequities and afflictions heaped upon them had to be dealt with and wisely eliminated. The requirements of the time and the conditions of the place, however, imposed certain limitations.

The pronouncement of the equality of the sexes, no matter how ideal and desirable, would have been impossible in those circumstances. The uncontrollable passions and lust-loving nature of the men of the day did not lend themselves to the practice of monogamy or to equal sharing of rights, privileges, and opportunities. The generality of men could only be pushed toward the requirements of spirituality to a certain degree. Therefore, the Prophet of God introduced steps to lessen the extent of the inhuman treatment of the women believers and revealed laws to improve their social and legal rights.

The Prophet Muḥammad abolished the practice of burying newly born girls alive, which was common among a certain clan. He did away with the inhuman treatment of

women who were taken captive in the incessant wars
which were waged by the tribes of Arabia. He institutionalized the marriage of Muslims. Within reasonable limits He
bestowed upon women the right to inherit and own proper-
ties legally. He admonished men to respect and love the
women who had given them birth and raised them. He exhorted husbands to be kind and just to their wives. He revealed spiritual laws and teachings to apply to His male and
female followers alike.

No other holy book had dealt in such detail with the affairs of women as did the Qur'an. In various suras, Muḥammad introduced many new laws intended to raise the status
of women and protect their rights. He says:

> The women ought also to behave towards their husbands
> in like manner as their husbands should behave towards
> them according to what is just . . .[10]

If we quote this passage of the Qur'an without making
reference to the continuation of the sentence, we can say
that at least in this particular case the Prophet Muḥammad
pronounced that men and women enjoy reciprocal rights in
relation to each other. But, alas, for certain reasons—one of
which was certainly the lack of men's capacity to deal with
such a revolutionary idea—He immediately disqualified the
women from equality by saying:

> . . . but the men ought to have a superiority over them
> . . .[11]

He went on to give men the right to divorce their wives,
and He admonished them thus:

> Ye may divorce your wives twice; and then either retain
> them with humanity, or dismiss them with kindness. But
> it is not lawful for you to take away anything of what ye

have given them, unless both fear that they cannot observe the ordinances of God . . .[12]

Here the Prophet sought to protect the rights of Muslim women in divorce. His admonition was grievously ignored in later Islamic practice.

In the following passage, Muḥammad exhorts His followers to respect the women who have borne them, to be equitable toward orphans who are girls, and to refrain from taking more than four wives. However, He advises that Muslim men should marry only one wife if they fear that they cannot act equitably toward more:

O men, fear your Lord, who hath created you out of one man, and out of him created his wife, and from the two hath multiplied many men and women: and fear God by whom ye beseech one another; and respect women, who have borne you, for God is watching over you . . . And if ye fear that ye shall not act with equity towards orphans of the female sex, take in marriage of such other women as please you, two, or three, or four, and not more. But if ye fear that ye cannot act equitably toward so many, marry one only . . .[13]

And yet, in the following passage, Muḥammad reveals further rules to govern relations between husband and wife, indicates the impossibility of observing equity between several women, emphasizes His abhorrence of divorce, and warns His male followers to fear God lest they abuse their wives:

If a woman fear ill usage, or aversion, from her husband, it shall be no crime in them if they agree the matter amicably between themselves; for a reconciliation is better than a separation. Men's souls are naturally inclined to covetousness: but if ye be kind towards women, and fear

to wrong them, God is well acquainted with what ye do.
Ye can by no means carry yourselves equally between
women in all respects, although ye study to do it; therefore turn not from a wife with all manner of aversion, nor
leave her like one in suspense: if ye agree, and fear to
abuse your wives, God is gracious and merciful . . .[14]

The matter of the veil (*hijáb*) advocated by the Prophet in
the Qur'an is another example of a pretext used by the followers of Muḥammad to impose endless restrictions on
women. The reason that the Prophet resorted to such a
device was to protect the women believers from the lusts
and passions of His male followers. But this, like every
other concession made to men in an effort to purge them of
their moral decay, was used as a further evidence of
women's worthlessness.

The veil was used by Muḥammad to admonish His male
followers concerning their dealing with His wives:

And when ye ask of the Prophet's wives what ye may
have occasion for, ask it of them from behind a curtain.
This will be more pure for your hearts and their hearts.[15]

Although the men are instructed to speak to Muḥammad's
wives from behind a curtain, He does not specify who, His
wives or the men, should be behind the curtain.

Addressing the rank and file of the believers, the Qur'an
says:

Speak unto the true believers, that they restrain their
eyes, and keep themselves from immodest actions: this
will be more pure for them; for God is well acquainted
with that which they do. And speak unto the believing
women, that they restrain their eyes, and preserve their
modesty, and discover not their ornaments, except what
necessarily appeareth thereof: and not show their orna-

ments, unless to their husbands, or their husbands' fathers, or their sons, or their husbands' sons, or their brothers, or their brothers' sons, or their sisters' sons, or their women, or the captives which their right hands shall possess, or unto such men as attend them, and have no need of women. . .[16]

In this passage, the exhortation to the believers to keep from immodest actions is directed toward men and women alike. Women are further required not to show their ornaments to the men, other than to the male members of their immediate families. It is the question of ornaments which is being discussed. They seem to have been a source of temptation to men, and in order to protect them from indecent promptings, the Prophet advises the women to conceal them.

In another passage, the Qur'an reads:

Men shall have the preeminence above women, because of those advantages wherein God hath caused the one of them to excel the other, and for that which they expend of their substance in maintaining their wives. The honest women are obedient, careful in the absence of their husbands, for that God preserveth them, by committing them to the care and protection of the men.[17]

This provides us with some insight into why the Prophet would countenance a disparity between the rights of men and women.

Unfortunately, the improved treatment of women believers in Islam began to erode soon after the Prophet's death. A review of the achievements of Muslim women in the early years of the Revelation compared to what became the lot of women in the Muslim world in the nineteenth century, prior to the Revelations of the Báb and Bahá'u'lláh, shows a steady decline in the status of women to a state similar to—if not worse than—what it was before Islam took hold. Religion was used to divest women of their rights and to reduce them to the position of inferior members of the human race.

The veil, for example, was used to keep the women in complete ignorance of whatever was going on beyond the boundaries of their homes. Discriminatory application of the laws of the Qur'an also resulted in the denial of education to women. 'Abdu'l-Bahá has said:

> *The status of woman in former times was exceedingly deplorable, for it was the belief of the Orient that it was best for woman to be ignorant. It was considered preferable that she should not know reading or writing in order that she might not be informed of events in the world. Woman was considered to be created for rearing children and attending to the duties of the household. If she pursued educational courses, it was deemed contrary to chastity; hence women were prisoners of the household. The houses did not even have windows opening upon the outside world.*[18]

In Islamic countries, the status of women reached such a degraded point that abusive language was commonly used to indicate the lowliness of their sex. The astonishing thing is the casual acceptance of such derogatory terms, which still prevails. In the words of 'Abdu'l-Bahá:

> *The community of women was so abased in the East that, in the Arabic language, when a mention was made of them in conversation one would say: "Far be it from thee to be a woman" as one would say: "Far be it from thee to be a donkey." In the Turkish language, it was said: "Exalted be thy presence from the mention of a woman." And in the Persian language, when talking about a woman one would say: "May there be no relationship"; moreover, the word "woman" was used as a synonym for "weak."*[19]

Equality in the Bahá'í Faith. The principle of the equality of men and women was proclaimed by Bahá'u'lláh, the Inaugurator of the Bahá'í Faith. He made the equitable treatment of the sexes one of His prerequisites for the administration of justice in the world. He states unequivocally:

> *All should know, and in this regard attain the splendors of the sun of certitude, and be illumined thereby: Women and men have been and will always be equal in the sight of God. The Dawning-Place of the Light of God sheddeth its radiance upon all with the same effulgence. Verily God created women for men, and men for women. The most beloved of people before God are the most steadfast and those who have surpassed others in their love for God, exalted be His glory.*[20]

Bahá'u'lláh revealed this principle of the equality of men and women at a time when womanhood had sunk to the lowest depths of misery and degradation. He recognized the agony of women and saw how they suffered by virtue of their sex. He beheld how women toiled in life without leaving name or trace. He observed in them the devotion that many men lacked, and He found in some of them a heroism that matched the bravest of all. He wanted the world to become aware of the capacity and worth of His female followers. In one Tablet He wrote:

> *Convey greetings on behalf of this Wronged One to all the handmaidens of that land and say: This is the day wherein the innermost gems of human reality must be made manifest. Strive, then, whilst there is yet time. He is verily the Trusted Admonisher.*[21]

In numerous Tablets, Bahá'u'lláh praised the courage and devoted services of the women believers and urged them to attain to loftier heights in upholding the interests of mankind. He removed every distinction that throughout the ages had given men their pretexts for subjugating women. The notion of the superiority of one sex over another He labeled an idle fancy. Bahá'u'lláh was the first Manifestation of God to enjoin the complete elimination of prejudice of sex. This is one of the striking features of His Faith that distinguishes it from the religions of the past. He writes:

> *Exalted, immensely exalted is He Who hath removed differences and established harmony. Glorified, infinitely glorified is He Who hath caused discord to cease, and decreed solidarity and unity. Praised be God, the Pen of the Most High hath lifted distinctions from between His servants and handmaidens and, through His consummate favors and all-encompassing mercy, hath conferred upon all a station and rank on the same plane. He hath broken the back of vain imaginings with the sword of utterance and hath obliterated the perils of idle fancies through the pervasive power of His might.*[22]

The pivotal aim of the Bahá'í Faith is the unity of humankind. It cannot, therefore, subscribe to the notions of superiority that were upheld by past religions because of the needs of a former time. How can a progressive religion advocate justice and yet wrong one half of the human race? Bahá'u'lláh has warned the oppressors of the earth to stay their hand from tyranny and has pledged Himself not to forgive any man's injustice.[23] In a Tablet addressed to one of the Bahá'í women of Iran, Bahá'u'lláh gives the assurance:

> *Soon will the pageantry of tyranny be rolled up and the panoply of justice unfolded as a bounty from the King of creation.*[24]

'Abdu'l-Bahá, as well, promoted the principle of the equality of men and women throughout his life. He revealed numerous Tablets calling on the women of the Faith to arise, achieve prominence and excellence in serving the Cause of God, acquire spiritual attributes, and manifest their potential. In many of His public talks and discourses, as well as in His writings, He emphasized this subject:

Male and female are one, and men and women are the same.[25]

They will prove that in this cycle women are equal to men, nay in certain respects they will excel.[26]

Divine justice demands that the rights of both sexes should be equally respected since neither is superior to the other in the eyes of Heaven.[27]

. . . woman has been outdistanced through lack of education and intellectual facilities. If given the same educational opportunities or course of study, she would develop the same capacity and abilities.[28]

While encouraging women to educate themselves in all fields of human endeavor, 'Abdu'l-Bahá lovingly exhorted them to avoid pitfalls that could hamper their progress. He warned them not to follow in the footsteps of the men who boasted of manual strength, prided themselves in thirst for conquest, and led mankind to contention and strife. 'Abdu'l-Bahá often exhorted the women of the East to follow the lead of their Bahá'í sisters in the West who had carried the Message of Bahá'u'lláh to far-off lands.

It is useful to contrast the forceful way in which 'Abdu'l-Bahá urged the Persian women of His time to arise, with the way in which Bahá'u'lláh had cautioned them, in His time, to refrain from such services as might be considered incompatible with traditional female roles. In one of the Tablets revealed in honor of a Bahá'í woman in Iran, Bahá'u'lláh writes:

O Hájar, forsake thy home for the love of God. That is, distance thyself from all that dwell on earth and repose beneath the Tree of divine love. Thou shalt thereby be reckoned as a migrant in the sight of God, even though thou mayest reside in thy home all thy life. Because in the eyes of God to forsake one's homeland is in fact a journey, not on foot but of the heart. With the permission of God, it is preferable to combine these two journeys—but this is for men, not for women. [29]

This temporary restriction on service to the Cause in the field of pioneering was completely removed at a later date by 'Abdu'l-Bahá, when the requirements of the time changed. 'Abdu'l-Bahá wrote:

O ye leaves who have attained certitude! In the countries of Europe and America the maidservants of the Merciful have won the prize of excellence and advancement from the arena of men, and in the fields of teaching and spreading the divine fragrances they have shown a brilliant hand. Soon they will soar like the birds of the Concourse on high in the far corners of the world and will guide the people and reveal to them the divine mysteries. Ye, who are the blessed leaves [i.e., the women] *from the East, should burn more brightly, and engage in spreading the sweet savors of the Lord and in reciting the verses of God. Arise, therefore, and exert yourselves to fulfill the exhortations and counsels of the Blessed Beauty, that all hopes may be realized and that the plain of streams and orchards may become the garden of oneness.* [30]

Likewise, there have been temporary restrictions placed upon women's service alongside men in some other areas, mainly in the field of Bahá'í Administration. The women in Iran continued to be circumscribed for some time. It was not until 1954, late in the ministry of the Guardian of the Bahá'í Faith, Shoghi Effendi, that Persian women were granted the right of membership on local and national Spiritual Assemblies.

The problem of educating men and women in Iran to champion the injunction of Bahá'u'lláh to equality was a colossal one. The male Bahá'ís did not exert much conscious effort to promote this aspect of the Teachings. When they talked about it, they were more apt to dwell on what 'Abdu'l-Bahá calls "minor differences" between men and women than on the abolition of male superiority. And it was as hard to bring the conscious awareness of this principle to the attention of the female believers as it was to the men. If Bahá'u'lláh had not firmly and explicitly revealed the principle of sexual equality, the oppression of women in the name of religion would certainly have continued in full force to this date.

Despite the fact that Tablets revealed by Bahá'u'lláh and 'Abdu'l-Bahá insist on equality, these Tablets were not disseminated among the believers in Iran until recent times. Women were generally illiterate before then and had to rely upon men to tell them what the Writings were about. In those days, men were little concerned with the needs of women. There was not sufficient appreciation of the stupendous importance of encouraging women to improve their status in preparation for equality. There are many Tablets which Bahá'u'lláh has revealed in honor of women believers which have to this day remained unpublished, even in the original language.

To expedite the advancement of women 'Abdu'l-Bahá encouraged several prominent Bahá'í women in the West to travel to Iran. Their services, which were rendered at great personal sacrifice and risk, served a twofold purpose. They demonstrated to the Bahá'í men that women were indeed capable of surpassing them in service to the Faith. They also showed the Bahá'í women that, once they rent asunder the veils intervening between them and their true selves, they would be able to educate themselves and achieve that which their Bahá'í sisters had attained in the West.

Bahá'ís have been struggling for nearly a century and a

half to bring the status of women up to the level of men. In some countries, genuine efforts by men and women to hasten the process of women's emancipation have borne favorable results. In other places, negligible efforts have been made and little progress realized. In a few countries the men cling fanatically to their traditional privileges and actively prevent women from developing their potential, delaying the realization of the ideal of the equality of men and women. Even this conscious resistance, however, shows that the men can no longer simply take their superior status for granted and indicates progress in the cause of womanhood.

Then there are some Bahá'ís who believe that since Bahá'u'lláh has willed the equality of men and women, it will no doubt be realized some time in the future—probably hundreds of years from now in the Golden Age of the Dispensation when humanity will have come fully of age and will have attained the zenith of its maturity. Of course, every follower of Bahá'u'lláh believes that this goal, like all of the other principles of the Cause, will be achieved in this Dispensation. The question is, however, how long men and women who are attached to the opposite way of life will create delay.

Those who have accepted the Cause are obliged to observe its provisions, including the implementation of every aspect of the equality of sexes. They also have the duty of studying the plight of women to determine where men went wrong in the past, so that their mistakes will not be repeated in this Cause. Any attempt by one sex to deny the rights of the other, no matter what the pretext, must be firmly repelled with justice. Even the tolerance of prejudiced attitudes toward one sex by another is detrimental to the full realization of the equality of men and women. Such tolerance only supports the oppression of women.

Women in Bahá'í History. In Iran, where the Bábí and Bahá'í religions have their root, as indeed in all Islamic countries in the nineteenth century, it was not considered honorable to write about women. Women were treated as a part of the possessions of the masculine head of every household. A woman's existence was only properly acknowledged, therefore, in relation to one or more of the male members of the family. Any attempt to discuss the events of a woman's life was interpreted as an intrusion on the privacy of that man, who had the prerogative of ensuring that the women of his household remained concealed and protected.

For these reasons, the painful plight of many early Bábí and Bahá'í women has escaped even the keen eye and the critical pen of Bahá'í historians, whose attitudes were so conditioned by the customary practices and unjust traditions of the time that they did not notice the struggles of most of the early women believers; or if they did, these appeared so insignificant to them that they did not warrant professional historical treatment.

But Bahá'í women have made major contributions to the development and spread of the Faith, especially in Iran. Their vast capacity for suffering in acquiescence placed them in an ideal position to render services of unsurpassed importance. Their self-effacement and self-sacrifice made them staunch believers who gave up all prospects of advancement in life to raise worthy children in the stronghold of the Cause. If their husbands were slain by the enemy for their religion and the children left without fathers—without home, shelter, support, or protection—the mothers immediately became their mainstay and shouldered, with remarkable strength, the demands of this new challenge. They toiled and suffered endless hardship, but they did not waver in their firm intent to keep the flame of the Faith burning in the breasts of their children. They achieved this by sacrificing everything that life had offered them. And they left behind them strong offspring who carried forward the vital work of the Faith, while their own services remained unrecognized and unsung.

History, unfortunately, does not reveal the full glory of the services of these early Bahá'í women. The constraints of the time and culture did not allow Bahá'í historians to record the accounts of the work of the female followers of the Faith. As a consequence, wide gaps have been left in the history of the Cause and the impression has been created that the early Bábí and Bahá'í women were just spectators to the major events of Bahá'í history. This painful absence of sufficient historical information about early women can, unfortunately, never be filled completely by modern historians because much has been lost forever. But more attention is certainly needed to illumine this aspect of Bahá'í history.

The Institutions of the New World Order. Women have been wronged and suffered unjustly in the past, not only because the principle of the equality of men and women was not clearly and firmly established by the Founders of religion, but also because the followers of past religions subscribed for various reasons to the notion of men's superiority. Inequities against women were presented as divinely ordained and their rights were undermined in the name of God.

Praised be God! This pretext does not exist in the Bahá'í Faith. The injunction of human equality that does away with distinctions of sex has been revealed with such clarity, and emphasized so forcefully, that any attempt to ignore it is rendered impossible and any misinterpretation is exposed as a conspicuous distortion of the truth. Once and for all, Bahá'u'lláh has obliterated the selfish causes that have given rise to the ascendancy of one sex over the other.

No individual or institution in the Bahá'í Faith has the right to abrogate what Bahá'u'lláh has explicitly revealed. The Universal House of Justice, the supreme institution of the Bahá'í Administrative Order, has the power to legislate in regard to matters not revealed by the Author of the Faith.

To this institution is also given the authority to elucidate those issues which are not clearly defined in the Writings.

Bahá'u'lláh speaks of the "men of the House of Justice." There are local, national, and international Houses of Justice. The membership of the international or Universal House of Justice, according to 'Abdu'l-Bahá, is limited to men only. The exclusion of women from membership on this Universal House of Justice may give rise to speculation that women's fate remains at the mercy of men even in this Dispensation—that their equality with men, acknowledged and confirmed by the Founder of the Faith, will soon suffer setbacks through legislation that will curtail their advancement.

Bahá'u'lláh has clearly stated that women and men have always been equal in the sight of God. However, the lessons of history, and specifically those of religious history, indicate the ruthless manner in which this basic principle of human reciprocity has been denied. Therefore, humanity has a right to look with skeptical eyes at the prospect of the full implementation of the Bahá'í program of equality of men and women and to voice concern about the possibility of the introduction of restrictions that will again push women into a position subordinate to men. It deserves to have proof that the exclusion of women from membership on the Universal House of Justice will not be used as a pretext to exclude them from membership on international executive and judicial institutions. A careful study of the Bahá'í Faith and the safeguards incorporated into its Administrative Order should remove the causes of any such apprehension.

The Universal House of Justice is a divinely ordained institution. Bahá'ís believe that it functions under the protection and guidance of Bahá'u'lláh and the Báb. It ensures that the Teachings of the Bahá'í Faith remain unadulterated; it promotes their fair enforcement; it protects the unity of the believers. The prime responsibility of the

House of Justice is to preserve the purity of Bahá'u'lláh's Revelation, and hence it legislates only when explicit reference is absent in the Writings. The principle of sexual equality is too explicit to be ignored in any deliberations.

Women's right to elect the members of the Universal House of Justice is another safeguard for ensuring respect for women in the deliberations of the House. Those members will be elected who are governed by the dictates of their conscience, rather than the interests of their sex. Femininity and masculinity will, therefore, never become an overriding concern in the area of legislation.

Both men and women enjoy the right to serve on the institutions of the future Bahá'í superstate. These institutions are referred to by Shoghi Effendi in his "Goal of a New World Order"[31] as an "International Executive," a "World Parliament," and a "Supreme Tribunal." In "The Unfoldment of World Civilization"[32] he speaks with more precision about a world commonwealth:

> . . . in which all nations, races, creeds and classes are closely and permanently united, and in which the autonomy of its state members and the personal freedom and initiative of the individuals that compose them are definitely and completely safeguarded. This commonwealth must, as far as we can visualize it, consist of a world legislature, whose members will, as the trustees of the whole of mankind, ultimately control the entire resources of all the component nations, and will enact such laws as shall be required to regulate the life, satisfy the needs and adjust the relationships of all races and peoples. A world executive, backed by an international Force, will carry out the decisions arrived at, and apply the laws enacted by, this world legislature, and will safeguard the organic unity of the whole world commonwealth. A world tribunal will adjudicate and deliver its

compulsory and final verdict in all and any disputes that may arise between the various elements constituting this universal system . . .[33]

Such institutions of a future world order do not carry the same restrictions with regard to their membership as does the Universal House of Justice. The judiciary and executive powers necessary to enforce the legislative are invested in institutions whose membership is open to women, inasmuch as there is no passage in the Writings barring them.

Although the exact nature of the relationship of the Supreme Tribunal to the world superstate cannot be foreseen, according to the letters of Shoghi Effendi, it is one aspect of that State. This indicates that the function of arbitration will be different from that of legislation. However, the Universal House of Justice, as the Supreme institution of the Bahá'í Administrative Order, will embrace the world tribunal, and the world executive, which "must aid and assist the legislative body."[34] Therefore, the anticipation that the international institutions of the world superstate will merge in the Universal House of Justice does not appear to convey the restriction that would exclude women from membership, especially since the statement by Shoghi Effendi about this merging was not made with regard to the membership of these institutions.

There are, however, Bahá'ís who maintain the assumption that whatever merges in the Universal House of Justice—such as the Supreme Tribunal—will necessarily exclude women from membership. But no reference can be found in the Writings of the Faith that would support such a claim. Those who maintain this position may, therefore, belong to the category of people who would rather hold on to the traditional notions of male superiority. Their supposition is that women will be obliged to accept exclusion from membership on a range of future institutions which constitute the executive and judicial bodies of a new world order.

The notion that women's exclusion from the Universal House of Justice may be extended to embrace other international institutions which are to be constituted in the future through the electoral process follows a pattern that has parallels in religious history. However, the absence of authentic references in Bahá'í Scripture that support such a possibility throws doubt on the soundness of such a highly speculative theory. Moreover, it contradicts 'Abdu'l-Bahá's prediction that women will enter all branches of administration. The only field that He has specifically reserved for men is that of the military—this because He says it is unworthy of women to participate in such activities. It is very difficult, generally speaking, for women to kill anyone. They confer life, and they cannot easily take it away.[35]

Women, according to the explicit text of the Writings of Bahá'u'lláh, are the first educators of children, and hence the first educators of mankind. To them is given the prime responsibility of overseeing and rearing the men from whose ranks the members of the House of Justice are elected, and the women from whose ranks come the mothers of those men, and ensuring that they will be properly educated to discharge their functions in the manner anticipated by Bahá'u'lláh. In the same way that parents, and especially mothers, are responsible for raising their children with equity and justice, the members of the Universal House of Justice are responsible for ensuring that the enactment of new laws will not be prejudicial towards either sex.

The permissibility of women's engagement in gainful employment is yet another means of removing the causes of masculine superiority found in the past. In Islam, as we have seen, the Qur'an granted preeminence to men that they might "expend of their substance in maintaining their wives." In the Bahá'í Dispensation, such advantages are completely obliterated in the interest of justice and equity. Women are granted the prerogative of earning a livelihood so that there may remain no cause for arguing the superiority of men. Bahá'u'lláh's statement is explicit and emphatic:

> *Everyone, whether man or woman, should hand over to a trusted person a portion of what he or she earneth through trade, agriculture or other occupations, for the training and education of children, to be spent for this purpose with the knowledge of the Trustees of the House of Justice.*[35]

Another safeguard to prevent the abuse of power by Bahá'í men is that the Universal House of Justice is deemed to be responsible to God when it deliberates on the affairs of the people. It is not a body answerable to the men and women who elect it. It has not been established to cater to the wishes of men, and it cannot legislate that which would betray the very reason for its existence—the administration of justice.

The equality of the sexes is an essential prerequisite for the realization of the unity of humankind, which is the basic principle and the ultimate aim of the Revelation of Bahá'u'lláh. The legislation of discriminatory practices against one half of humanity would certainly affect the unity of humanity as a whole. This would, in turn, defeat the very purpose of Bahá'u'lláh's Revelation—the establishment of universal peace.

The Universal House of Justice is the abrogator of the laws that it creates. The exigency of the times during the early stages of the development of the Bahá'í community may require that the enforcement of equal rights, equal privileges, and equal opportunities for men and women be implemented gradually. If so, at a later time when such conservatism is no longer needed, changes will no doubt be introduced to ensure the full achievement of that distinguishing feature of this Revelation.

It rests with the believers in the Faith to meet the challenge and to prove to the world that, although men and women are given specific functions which they may be intrinsically best suited to perform, they are nonetheless equal beneficiaries of the bounties which are vouchsafed to them from one and the same Creator. Together they can mirror forth the perfections of humanity in their full splendor.

The question in this Dispensation is not whether the equality of men and women is possible. It is rather whether women will arise and acquire what is rightfully theirs. Women, as human beings enjoying the blessing of free will, are endowed with the capacity to reclaim and achieve that which has been unjustly usurped from them in the past. Victory in the women's struggle will not be achieved through the futile methods that men employ to maintain their superiority and oppression. It will come, rather, through making the utmost use of the intellectual faculty, and in adherence to the exhortations enshrined in the Writings.

God has in this age commanded the unity of the people and has revealed, through the pen of His Manifestation Bahá'u'lláh, the principle of the equality of the sexes. He has made the necessary provisions to ensure that women will no longer be wronged by men. However, our conscious efforts in bringing about this glorious end will, to a large degree, determine the time span within which full equality will be established.

Notes

1. 'Abdu'l-Bahá, *Paris Talks* (London: Bahá'í Publishing Trust, 10th Ed., 1961) p. 161.

2. 'Abdu'l-Bahá, *The Promulgation of Universal Peace*, comp. by Howard MacNutt (Wilmette, Ill.: Bahá'í Publishing Committee, 1943) p. 133.

3. Gen. 1:27.

4. Gen. 3:16.

5. 'Abdu'l-Bahá, *Some Answered Questions* (Wilmette, Ill.: Bahá'í Publishing Trust, 1981) p. 123.

6. 1 Cor. 11:3.

7. 1 Cor. 14:34.

8. 1 Tim. 2:11–15.

9. 1 Cor. 11:6–9.

10. *The Qur'an*, trans. by George Sale (London: Frederick Warne and Co.) p. 32.

11. Ibid.

12. Ibid.

13. Ibid., p. 71.

14. Ibid., p. 91.

15. Ibid., pp. 416–17.

16. Ibid., pp. 346–47.

17. Ibid., p. 77.

18. 'Abdu'l-Bahá, *The Promulgation of Universal Peace*, p. 166.

19. 'Abdu'l-Bahá. Not previously translated. See *Makátíb-i 'Abdu'l-Bahá*, Vol. 7 (Tehran: Bahá'í Publishing Trust, 134 B.E.) pp. 93–94.

20. Bahá'u'lláh. Not previously translated.

21. Bahá'u'lláh. Not previously translated.

22. Bahá'u'lláh, quoted in *Women: Extracts from the Writings of Bahá'u'lláh, 'Abdu'l-Bahá, Shoghi Effendi, and the Universal House of Justice* (Thornhill, Ont.: Bahá'í Canada Publications, 1986) p. 2.

23. Bahá'u'lláh, *The Hidden Words*, trans. by Shoghi Effendi (Wilmette, Ill.: Bahá'í Publishing Committee, 1943) Persian #64.

24. Bahá'u'lláh. Not previously translated.

25. 'Abdu'l-Bahá. Not previously translated. See *Makátíb-i 'Abdu'l-Bahá*, p. 64. This sentence reflects a formula of language used to emphasize something beyond a shadow of a doubt.

26. 'Abdu'l-Bahá, quoted in *Women*, p. 48.

27. 'Abdu'l-Bahá, *Paris Talks*, pp. 161–62.

28. 'Abdu'l-Bahá, *The Promulgation of Universal Peace*, pp. 180–81.

29. Bahá'u'lláh. Not previously translated.

30. 'Abdu'l-Bahá, quoted in *Women*, p. 46.

31. Shoghi Effendi, in *The World Order of Bahá'u'lláh* (Wilmette, Ill.: Bahá'í Publishing Trust, 1938) pp. 29–48.

32. Shoghi Effendi, in *The World Order of Bahá'u'lláh*, pp. 161–206.

33. Ibid., p. 203.

34. 'Abdu'l-Bahá, *The Will and Testament of 'Abdu'l-Bahá* (Wilmette, Ill.: Bahá'í Publishing Trust, 1944) p. 15.

35. 'Abdu'l-Bahá, *Paris Talks*, p. 182.

36. Bahá'u'lláh, *Tablets of Bahá'u'lláh* (Haifa: Bahá'í World Centre, 1978) p. 90.

Recovering a Lost Horizon: Women's Contributions to North American Bahá'í History

by R. Jackson Armstrong-Ingram

A QUICK GLANCE ALONG THE SHELVES of a well-stocked Bahá'í library might suggest that Western Bahá'ís are reasonably well acquainted with the contributions of women to the history of their Faith. There is a diary, a collection of writing, and some biographical treatments, dealing with the lives and work of such women as Martha Root, Dorothy Baker, Lua Getsinger, Juliet Thompson, and Lidja Zamenhof. But such an impression would be misleading.

This handful of women has been singled out for published treatment largely on the basis of a feminized version of the "great men" theory of history. By definition they are viewed as having been exceptional to have warranted such treatment. (They are also exceptional in that they were mostly unmarried, or if married, childless.) There have been some briefer treatments of the contributions of individual women in periodicals and in the "In Memoriam" sections of the

Copyright © 1987 by R. Jackson Armstrong-Ingram. I wish to acknowledge the assistance given to my on-going research by a grant-in-aid from The Victory Foundation.

volumes of *The Bahá'í World*. Again, most of these women
are portrayed as being individually exceptional, even if the
tendency toward hagiography in some of these pieces results
in a rather standardized portrayal of exceptionality.

When the development of Bahá'í communities and institutions has been discussed in corporate terms in Bahá'í history,
the role of women has not been given due consideration.
There are three major areas of women's Bahá'í activity
which are largely undiscussed by historians and which
deserve serious study. First, the involvement of women in
the development of Bahá'í organization and the influence
they had on that development, through their participation in
both gender-segregated and -integrated bodies; second, the
existence of important networks of cooperation, support, and
patronage among early Bahá'í women; third, the contribution
of Bahá'í women to the early intellectual development of
their Faith in America through the teaching of an esoteric
and secret women's doctrine.

This brief discussion will do no more than introduce these
three neglected areas of Bahá'í history. I plan to discuss
them in considerably more detail on a future occasion and so
will reserve detailed illustration and documentation until
then. My current purpose is simply to draw attention to the
need to broaden the parameters of Bahá'í historical study.

The discussion of the first two decades of the Bahá'í Faith
in North America has often been distorted by excessive focus
on developments in Chicago, and especially on the all-male
Chicago House of Justice (later designated, House of Spirituality). That this should be so is not surprising. In many ways
Chicago—with its House of Spirituality—was the center of
the early community; but in at least as many ways it was not.

The situation of the Bahá'í community in Chicago in those
years was not the situation of all Bahá'í communities in
North America. However, the development of the Chicago
House of Spirituality has been the most adequately and ac-
cessibly documented aspect of that early period. Most histories of the early community do mention the obvious fact that

developments in the New York Bahá'í community, and in particular those associated with its Board of Counsel, were comparable in scale and importance to those in Chicago. Nevertheless, the comparative dearth of documentation available on the New York Board has prevented comparable discussion of developments there.

It is well known that winners write history. One reason they do is that the records generated by winners are more likely to survive than the records generated by losers. Winners have descendants who are in a position to protect their heritage and who have reason to want to do so. In the case of Chicago: The local Bahá'í institution that developed and stabilized there in the 1920s, the Spiritual Assembly of the Bahá'ís of Chicago, claimed direct descent from the Chicago House of Spirituality. A member of that institution had previously been a member of the House of Spirituality and had been concerned with amassing and protecting documentation about it almost from its inception. This has given the Chicago House an enormous advantage of visibility in the Bahá'í history of Chicago and North America. That the Chicago House was also seen as in some way ancestral to the National Spiritual Assembly has further reinforced this advantage.

The Chicago House of Spirituality undoubtedly had an important role, but the immense imbalance between the documentation available on it and that for any other Bahá'í organization in Chicago or North America during the same time period results in a tendency to conceptualize the early history of the Bahá'í Faith on this continent in terms of that one body. Since this institution was composed solely of men until 1912, the role of women in early Bahá'í history—insofar as later developments have tended to make general (as opposed to biographical) Bahá'í history institution-oriented—is seen as either supporting or opposing the Chicago House. A House-centered history of the first two decades of the Bahá'í Faith in North America is almost of necessity a history that must see women either as followers or as irritants. It is generally the irritants of such a history that become the heroines of the biographies, for the women of the biographies (with the partial exception of Dorothy Baker) did not tend to be institutional. They labored on the periphery of institutional structures toward individual ends.

In the generalized accounts, men "are" history: They create the structures of history itself. In the biographies, particular women act within history: Their activities are tangential to the historical structure created by men. As women were actually in the majority in the Bahá'í community (as they usually are in religious movements in North America), this approach relegates the experiences and endeavors of most Bahá'ís of the time to a position of residual importance in the history of the Faith. It allows for a few exceptions to be memorialized, but the "core" of the "real" history is the development of a minority-controlled institutional structure. Even for Chicago, this results in a biased picture. If we look more closely at the Bahá'í community in Chicago itself, we find that as well as the House of Spirituality there was also a Women's Assembly of Teaching. This parallel women's institution is documented only in a very fragmentary way, but nonetheless it can be seen to have had an institutional existence of some vigor. To date, discussion of the Women's Assembly of Teaching has mostly portrayed it as an auxiliary to the House, which was undoubtedly what the House wished it to be. It would probably be more accurate, however, to view it as a parallel institution of comparable significance in the local community. In New York also, there was some development of a women's institution parallel to the men's Board. We might note further that although women voted in the elections for the all-male bodies, men did not vote in the elections for the women's institutions.

Such segregated developments in these two cities have mistakenly been seen as evidence of a general tension in the national community over whether women could serve on Bahá'í administrative institutions. Such tension was of importance for developments in Chicago and New York, but in many other communities men and women served together from the inception of Bahá'í organization. The question then emerges: Why was there such obvious gender tension in the process of developing Bahá'í institutions in Chicago and New York, and not in many other places?

Certainly, one thing that both permitted and encouraged this tension in Chicago was that the House of Spirituality was regarded as different from all other local community organizations in the country. This enabled it to claim that special standards should apply to its composition and function. The Chicago House had been set up, in part, by Mirza Assad'Ullah who (in common with other Eastern Bahá'í teachers) had informed the Chicago community that according to Bahá'í scripture women could not serve on such a body. This was probably not ill-received by a number of the men (and women), who were naturally products of their time and place. That many of the efforts toward local organization that developed subsequently were seen as being at a pre-House-of-Spirituality stage of development, and thus lower in status than the Chicago House (although they were actually doing much the same things at the local level), seems to have meant that there was no attempt to suggest that the "organizationally inferior" sex could not serve on these inferior institutions. At any rate, the surviving records of a number of smaller communities show that they peaceably elected mixed bodies from the beginning; and in different years they elected men and women to the same institutional positions.

Another factor in encouraging gender tension in Chicago was the size of the city and the community. Working hours in the early 1900s were considerably longer than is normally the case today. If we add to these long hours, spread over a five-and-a-half or six-day week, the travel time needed to get to and from work in a large city, men simply did not have much time to be active in the Faith. Some men who did give considerable time to it suffered reverses in their careers or businesses. One was given the choice by his employer of spending less time on work for the Faith or accepting a demotion and transfer; he chose the latter. This time pressure seems to have led to some jealousy toward women. They were seen as being able to find time to meet during the day—perhaps on several days a week—and thus could do more to teach and study the Faith than men could.

That women could do more, and in doing more bring more women into the Faith, was regarded as a threat to the rational control of the development of the movement, as this could only be provided by institutions which had been defined as limited to men. Around 1910, there was considerable concern to encourage men to teach and bring more men into the Faith, as they were felt to be desperately needed. One of the aims of establishing *Bahá'í News* (later, *Star of the West*) in that year was to provide such encouragement on a national basis.

Thus, the social pressures on men that limited their ability to work for the Faith and the widespread belief of the time in the inherent irrationality of women, along with Middle-Eastern prejudice (that was supposedly supported by Bahá'í scripture), combined to create a situation where women's capacity to organize might be viewed as a threat to the long-term interests of the Faith. For women to organize themselves while there was no established network of men's institutions to "control" them, was to risk the creation of an inherently irrational institutional structure for the Faith.

In the smaller communities, there was obviously no travel difficulty such as existed in metropolitan areas. The surviving records also suggest that the men who joined the Faith in these communities did not feel the same level of gender tension that at least some of the more prominent men in the larger communities did. The holding of segregated meetings (this being easily done by manipulating the time of meetings to exclude most men) does not seem to have been a common factor in these smaller communities either.

It should be acknowledged that the feelings of some of the men in Chicago were not entirely due to paranoia. Although women did have work of their own to do in the home (and some outside it) that probably added up to a number of hours roughly equivalent to that of a man's working week, they did often have more flexibility as to when they did it. Also, that they did their work at home, and those homes were often in the same neighborhoods as some other Bahá'í women, not only saved them traveling time but enabled them to substitute Bahá'í meetings for normal afternoon visiting. Thus, in the latter half of the first decade of this century, of the thirteen meetings held each week in homes in Chicago, nine were hosted by women and took place in the afternoon. Of the other four, three were hosted by two married couples and two of these meetings were in the evening. (Only one meeting was hosted solely by a man, a widower, and it was in the evening.) There was also an afternoon "Nineteen-Day Tea" held regularly by the Women's Assembly.

There was one attempt to adapt an established pattern of men's social interaction to Bahá'í purposes. A small group of Bahá'í businessmen met regularly for lunch in a particular restaurant. The most notable result from this practice was the inception of the Bahá'í Publishing Society, the idea for which was raised at one of these meetings.

Another factor that operated to women's advantage was that the upper level of the social spectrum of Bahá'í women was above that of the men. This resulted in class factors mixing with gender tension. Bahá'í women as a group had more material resources, and the freedom that goes with them, at their disposal, than men. We may mention here also that some disputes among individuals articulated in gender terms were at least as much personality clashes that coincidentally crossed gender lines. Lastly, we may note there were some women (and men) who opposed all organization per se.

In many smaller communities, then, the beginnings of local organization within the Faith developed in a gender-integrated fashion, while in Chicago and New York there developed women's institutional structures parallel to the men's structures. These latter, certainly in the case of Chicago at least, should not be seen as merely oppositional in nature but as having a rationale of their own and interacting with the men's structures with varying degrees of cordiality. In particular, the organizing of large scale community events, such as Holy Day celebrations, was often a joint effort. We have seen also, that the segregated nature of the process of institutionalization in Chicago both encouraged and fed on a tendency toward gender segregation in Bahá'í community life there. This does not seem to have been so prevalent in the smaller communities.

Beyond this dynamic of segregated versus integrated institutional structures, however, there was the development of more specifically women's structures in the Bahá'í community. One feature of the early Western Bahá'í community was its interest in the Eastern Bahá'ís. This was expressed in a number of ways, including the exchange of correspondence between individuals and institutions of the two communities. Toward the end of the first decade of the century, an attempt was made to organize communication between the women of the Eastern and Western communities in a more structured way through the inauguration of a "Unity Band." Under this scheme, a woman was appointed in each of a number of places in North America to be responsible for corresponding with the women of a particular community in the East as a representative of Western

Bahá'í women. The replies from the East were then to be widely circulated. This scheme did supply Western Bahá'í women with a degree of intimate contact with their Eastern counterparts for awhile, informing them of their experiences and concerns, and it had good potential for deepening such contacts as had existed previously. However, the plan seems to have been a victim of the general malaise that beset the community around 1910, and which lasted into the middle of the second decade of the century. During these years, much organized activity lost momentum.

The impulses toward East-West cooperation among women expressed in the Unity Band were also behind the support given to the Tarbiat-ol-Benat (Girls' School) established in Tehran around the same time. This grew to be a highly respected school with the assistance of American Bahá'í women as resident teachers and concerned, though geographically distant, financial supporters. (I have discussed this in more detail elsewhere.*) It was further expressed in the much less successful plan to endow a girls' school in Haifa.†

The Unity Band and the schools, with their aims of encouragement and assistance, exemplify on the international level a feature of the lives of Bahá'í women within North America itself—patronage. Patronage networks in the early community were of considerable importance. They ranged from a single housewife teaching the Faith to her cleaning woman and then sponsoring her as a new Bahá'í, to extended and interrelated groups of clients dependent to varying degrees on one wealthy and influential patroness.

---

*R. Jackson Armstrong-Ingram, "American Bahá'í Women and the Education of Girls in Tehran," in *Studies in Bábí and Bahá'í History, Volume Three: In Iran* (Los Angeles: Kalimát Press, 1986) pp. 181–210.

†See *Munírih Khánum: Memoirs and Letters* (Los Angeles: Kalimát Press, 1986) pp. 77–81.

There were a few men who operated as patrons in the early community, but men's patronage was limited by the relative lack of wealthy and leisured individuals among them. Nor does the penetration of men's networks into the community and into their participants' lives seem to have been as extensive. The few wealthy men seem generally to have been inclined to spend money for the Faith doing things themselves, rather than through clients.

Given the small number of Bahá'ís in the early North American community, there was a mere handful of women who could function as patronesses in the extended sense but the number of clients that each of these women had was considerable. The degree of reliance varied from small favors, to help with emergency expenses (such as surgery), to full financial support of varying degrees of permanence. On one occasion, a client of an important patroness was kept busy visiting two other clients, who were hospitalized for surgery on different floors of the same hospital, and submitting reports on their welfare to their mutual benefactress.

Clientage networks gave patronesses considerable prestige in the community—and indeed power. Whether certain teaching trips were made, events held, books published—and even the quality and length of individual lives—could depend on them. However, this was rarely known in its specifics beyond selected members of their client group. The question of the influence of these women in the Bahá'í community is a complex one. They were of a social position that would have commanded respect in itself. But it seems likely that, while the full extent of their financial support of the community was often not widely known, they acquired an added aura of prestige through the praises of their clientage network. Certainly, it was mainly these women who were elected or appointed to positions of national prominence and overt influence and there are instances where their opinions had considerable general effect.

The clients of these women did include some men. But they were generally related to women clients, sponsored by women clients, or in some way marginal to the general men's community. For the women who were clients of the few large-scale patronesses, their common point of reliance seems to have been the significant bond. The clients of a patroness were from different social strata and do not seem to have viewed each other as social equals, but they did have a common bond in their network participation. That these networks had a lateral as well as vertical function can be seen from the number of different clients who might be involved in discussing how best to assist one of their number and in the fact that established clients were often aware of what help others were being given.

Clients would also assist each other in various ways. As with the hospital visitor, a client might do things for another client on the patroness's behalf with any expenses being refunded to her, but with her giving her own time and energy to another member of the network. These women's clientage networks also provided a forum to discuss problems which, given the ethos of the time, probably could not have been discussed with an institution on which men served (such as the Chicago House or a local Board)— problems such as marital difficulties or whether or not to have an abortion.

The women who functioned as large-scale patronesses in the Bahá'í community in these early years were of a social position where such activity was normally expected of them. Their patronage in the Bahá'í community was an extension of their general social role. Within the community it had the added effect of bringing together Bahá'í women of different classes and towns, and helping to create a consciousness of belonging to a national rather than merely a local Bahá'í community.

Another women's network of importance in the early North American Bahá'í community was concerned with esoteric teachings. The early Western Bahá'ís had limited access to the writings of their Faith, although this access was nowhere near as limited as is sometimes portrayed, especially by 1910. In addition, there was no established body of theological comment available to them. The nineteenth century had seen in North America the growth of much creative thought on the position of women in society. By the latter part of the century, this thought constituted a loosely-knit nexus. This nexus of ideas drew on many sources, from transcendentalism to social reform movements, and had itself some effect on the general ideological conception of women in North America. The thought of some early Bahá'í women was influenced by this nexus. Out of it, and based on their understanding of the Bahá'í Faith derived from such texts as were available to them and from interviews with early Persian teachers, these women developed an esoteric Bahá'í theology. It was esoteric in that it was taught only to women, and only to women who were judged to be able to comprehend it.

This woman's theology played an important part in enabling those who were inducted into it to imbue their social roles with religious content. It elaborated on the "work is worship" theme of Bahá'í teaching to develop a concept of the socially reconstitutive power of "service." At a more abstract level, it presented a gender-integrated concept of the deity and provided a symbology within which individual devotional and mystical experience might be structured.

There seem to have been degrees of initiation into the full theology, as there are a number of instances where women obviously knew something of it, but just as evidently did not comprehend it in detail. There are also a very few cases where men seem to have had some surface knowledge of the symbols used in the women's theology. However, it does not seem likely that any man was more fully acquainted with it than this. In its fullest expression, this women's theology was probably the first elaborated theological consideration of the teachings of the Bahá'í Faith by Western minds to go beyond the theme of prophecy.

An interesting point about the esoteric network is that it operated mainly at the middle level of the women of the community. It does not seem to have included the most important patronesses, but was concentrated at the level of those who were more likely to be clients. Thus, cutting through the network of material patronage there was a network of intellectual patronage: Members of the latter often participated in the former, but the former as a whole was not acquainted with the teachings circulating in the latter. The esoteric network also permitted at the intellectual level what the patronage network permitted at the material level—the consideration of issues that would have been difficult to discuss in mixed company at the time. In particular, that it was limited to women permitted the use of an explicitly sexual symbology.

In the first two decades of the Bahá'í Faith in North America, then, women were involved in three main areas of specifically women's group endeavor. They participated in the organization of the Faith, in an integrated way in many communities, and in parallel women's institutions where this was necessary; they participated in the Bahá'í social program through moves toward East-West cooperation and support, and through the patronage network; and they participated in the intellectual development of the Faith in the West through an esoteric philosophical network.

As the Faith continued to develop in the teens of this century and beyond, it is evident that the first of these areas of participation remained important—especially as the practice of gender segregation in administrative institutions died out. Nevertheless, gender tension in the institutional situation continued. Women remained a majority in the Faith, but were a minority in the institutional power structure at the national level. Those women who were elected to national office came from the upper levels of society and were not typical of the women of the community. In the work of the Faith at the national level, there was still an element of segregation. Although the National Assembly was mostly men, the actual work of most national committees was accomplished by women (even if there were men on the committee). Thus, establishing goals and announcing their achievement was the prerogative of an Assembly of mostly men, but the actual achieving was most often the work of women—on the committees and in the community generally.

The extent to which women assumed the actual work of the Faith may be seen from the ratio of women to men in those positions actually responsible for doing the work.* On national committees, there is a distinction between the ratio for the post of chairman and for that of secretary. Thus in 1937, the ratio for chairman was 1.9 and that for secretary was 12. The ratio for secretary varies widely over the years—both up and down, but it is always appreciably higher than that for chairman. At the level of regional teaching committees, the ratio for secretary was also 12 in 1937. In that same year, the ratio for Local Assembly secretaries was 4.83.

The degree to which women did the work at the local level increased over the years. The ratio for the post of local secretary rises steadily; by 1958, it was 11.5 and in 1968, it was 18.95. Whatever these ratios may also indicate about the gender stereotypes that members of Bahá'í Assemblies brought to the election of their secretaries, they amply demonstrate the extent to which the work of the local communities was disproportionately carried by women. In contrast to the local situation, we may note that, despite the ratios for national committee secretaries, there has never been a woman elected to the post of National Assembly secretary.

*In the following, the figure 1 means one woman to one man; 2 means two women to one man; and so on.

In the field of teaching, a convenient source for considering the level of women's contribution at a particularly active time is the lists published in *Bahá'í News* (Nos. 161,
164, 167) of those who pioneered or did extended travel
teaching in North America between the National Convention in 1942 and October 1943. This was a period during
which there was considerable encouragement to meet the
community's goals prior to the celebration of the centenary
of the Declaration of the Báb in 1944. Because of the scale
of effort needed to feature in these lists, they should represent the bulk of the most active and committed of those
teaching the Faith in North America at that time.

For those who pioneered to "virgin" states and provinces
in the United States and Canada, the ratio of women to
men was 5.22. For those who pioneered to restore dis-
banded Assemblies the ratio was 2.78. For those who did
extended travel teaching the ratio was 3. Arguments are
sometimes raised to suggest that it was easier for women
to engage in such activities than for men. They did not
have to support families; they did not have to be as concerned with the development of a "career," etc. But this
does not alter the fact that, here too, a disproportionately
high amount of the work was being done by women and
that they were more likely than men to choose the more
arduous posts.

Another area of gender tension at the national level, particularly in the 1930s, was between the national Bahá'í administrative structure and a number of individual Bahá'í
women who traveled across the country teaching the Faith
in their own fashion. Some of these women were from the
upper strata of society and had substantial resources at
their disposal; others earned the money they needed as
they went along. What the wealthy women were doing was
similar to what men of their position had tended to do
earlier. But the men had done it at a time when there was
not a well-developed national administration, and when the
beginnings of such an administration had been dominated

by men. That some of these women did cause problems is true, but almost beside the point. Nationally approved and sponsored teachers were capable of causing just as many. The issue was mainly one of control and, as the "problem" concerned the activities of women, it assumed a gender dimension. We may note here that many of the approved teachers were also women.

The involvement of women in the second area of activity —social programs and patronage—also continued after the teens but in increasingly disguised forms. We have seen that the concern with the Eastern community continued through the Tarbiat-ol-Benat, but organized contact through direct correspondence with the women of the Eastern community was not revived. The much longer-lasting practice of correspondence between local institutions of the Faith in the East and the West also died out due, at least in part, to an increasingly hierarchical view of Bahá'í institutions that saw international correspondence as inappropriate for local bodies.

Changes in North American society after the First World War affected patronage generally, as modern social institutions took over much of its role. Within the Bahá'í community, there were instances of Bahá'ís involving themselves in such general activities for social betterment as soup kitchens, prison visiting and reform, and educational developments. The old-style, personal patronage continued but gradually became the exceptional case. The patronesses continued to give substantially to the work of the Faith, but over time such giving became more and more integrated into the developing administrative structure. Money for activities such as a teaching tour could now be channeled through an established fund and could be contributed without a specific recipient in mind. Other activities, such as conferences and publishing, also became integrated into the Bahá'í administrative system.

The personal-assistance level of patronage did remain to

an extent but, as concern for health and welfare became more generally institutionalized in society, the need for it seemed less if there were no preexisting connection to suggest it. In the 1940s, when an active full-time worker for the Faith became ill and required care she could not afford, the National Spiritual Assembly assisted and acted as a channel for assistance. Thirty years earlier such assistance would have been given as an act of individual patronage.

Patronage channeled through the administrative system, however, could retain a personal dimension. Funds might be earmarked for specific purposes or recipients. Even more specifically, some women negotiated donations directly with the women of the particular committee that wished to use their contribution, and the treasury of the National Assembly was merely used as a bookkeeping service. Over time, however, general knowledge of such acts of individual patronage became unusual, and the publicly acknowledged source of patronage was usually the national treasury.

Developments in the third area of participation, the esoteric network, are by their very nature harder to discuss. Actual induction into the network may have continued at least into the 1920s; it is difficult to say. However, influences from it recur well into the 1940s, and even the 1950s. The women who were part of the network in the early years of the century often remained active in the Faith for the rest of their lives, and it is unlikely that those who were fully acquainted with the esoteric theology were unaffected by it in their later activities. Fragmentary aspects of the esoteric teaching may be found being passed on to younger women in advice until the early 1950s. To what extent these fragments represented a true survival of remnants of the teaching, or to what extent they reflected the general women's culture of North American society, is unclear.

Probably what most limited the survival of the women's

theology was its secrecy. As part of the development of Bahá'í administration through the 1920s and 1930s, there arose considerable distrust of any attempt to stand apart from the generality of Bahá'ís or to depart from the institutionally approved picture of the Faith. The whole tenor of developments within the Faith during this time in North America militated against esotericism, mysticism, and abstract theological speculation. In part, this was due to the great emphasis being placed on centralization and hierarchical control. In part, it resulted from the new presentation of Bahá'í teachings as basically a social program. It also specifically reflected the experience of the administration with the New History Society, a breakaway faction.

The fullness of the women's theology was probably quietly lost to the community death by death during those years. Whether by the 1940s any woman, who had not been an adult before 1910, was acquainted with the esoteric teaching in depth is doubtful.

The overseas teaching responsibilities of the North American Bahá'í community which began in the mid-1930s, and developed in the 1940s and 1950s, helped to complete the changes in the nature of that community that were already under way. The dual tendencies toward centralization and the presentation of a simplified and practical picture of the Faith were reinforced by the demands of establishing communities in other countries, with other languages, and with different cultures. In this endeavor too, much of the work was done by women: at home on committees and overseas as pioneers. The tensions in the administrative structure during this period came to the point that a woman member of the National Assembly gave her primary loyalty to the committee on which she also sat in areas of the committee's concern. She submitted to the committee's guidance as to what information she should disclose to the Assembly regarding the committee's business, rather than feeling herself bound as an Assembly

member to share with that body all she knew of relevance
to their decision making.

The push to establish Bahá'í communities overseas in the
1940s and 1950s, removed many of the most active Bahá'ís
from the North American community. Their contem-
poraries came to feel that the community had been drained
of many of its resources. This was expressed in the greater
difficulty there was felt to have been in acheiving home
front goals in the latter part of this period. The United
States community recovered from the demands of the overseas work, and could concentrate more on its own expan-
sion, from the early 1960s. The earlier depletion of the
community's energy through an extended period of send-
ing many of its most active members overseas, and the
later recovery, has had the effect of creating a present community that is in many ways adrift from its past.

In the 1920s, despite the community's clear direction, it
still had within it the knowledge of its earlier self and an
awareness of options open to it other than those it was currently exercising. After all, a reasonable proportion of the
community's members had been so since the earlier days,
when the concerns and interests of Bahá'ís were broader.
With the removal of this consciousness (through death
from old age, and through pioneering by many of those who
had passed their youth in the early community or who had
been taught by its members during the 1930s–1950s), the
community's knowledge of itself and its options drew in.
Throughout the 1960s, 1970s, and 1980s, the Faith in
North America developed on the basis of a more limited
range of possibilities than the early community had known.
Needs in the areas of devotions, teaching, and administration were felt and expressed without any realization that
they had once been successfully met. Access to much of the
community's accumulated experience had been lost. The
seeds of the new Faith, which had blown across an ocean
and grown wild, developing different strains in different

circumstances, had been domesticated. They were now sown with all the attendant dangers of monoculture.

One of the most important strains to be lost was the knowledge of women's structures and ideology. It is vital that we recover that lost horizon—not because there is some specific fascination to the manifestations of women's minds; not that knowledge of these aspects of our past is useful only to lend charm, or period color, or spice up the institutional history. But because women's thoughts and actions helped shape the institutional history as much as men's did, and we cannot understand that without being concerned with them. Because they represented the response of a specific culture to the Bahá'í Faith, a response which differed from the response of men's culture, and we need to consider as many reponses to the Revelation as we can to help us formulate our own response. And because gender tensions exist within the Bahá'í community today, and we need to know the history of these tensions and the previous responses to them to be able to work toward a Bahá'í culture beyond them.

With the exception of those mentioned in the first paragraph, I have intentionally not named any women (or men) in this essay. This is not because individuals are not important, and not because there are not individual and personal aspects to history. But when a society establishes groups within itself, and on the basis of ascription to those groups defines matters of status and personal options, each of these groups develops—to some extent—a culture and structure of its own. This culture and structure is not inherent in the individuals who make up such groups, but is a function of the society that has delimited them. When the Bahá'í Faith was introduced to the West, both the society to which it came and its own structural development delimited women as a distinct group. Society was divided on gender lines, and the Bahá'í Faith was conceptualized as reinforcing that dichotomy.

The books I mentioned in the first paragraph of this essay are primarily concerned with individuals who are portrayed, in the main, as coincidentally having been women. My concern has been to point out some aspects of Bahá'í women's culture and structure which were established in relation to the dichotomization of society and the Faith and which had (and have) a context beyond the individual. I believe that the consideration of these aspects is of importance for understanding where we have come from and our options for where we go from here. It is also evident, although the specifics of this essay refer to the Bahá'í community in North America, its basic thrust is applicable on a wider scale in this gender-dichotomized world.

Two Career Couples

by Judy A. Maddox

TODAY, IN THE United States, it is estimated that there are fifteen million families in which both parents work outside the home. In households with only one parent, over 70% must work outside of the home to support the family. In all, there are about nineteen million women with children in either full- or part-time employment.¹ This figure represents almost 60% of all the mothers in the country. These staggering statistics demonstrate that the nuclear family, as portrayed in the media throughout the '50s, '60s and '70s (i.e., father as breadwinner and mother as full-time homemaker) is fading into obscurity. More than 50% of married mothers and 79% of divorced mothers are in the work force. This means that 56% of the nation's fifty-eight million children have working moms.²

Long before inflation and social change pushed the nuclear family to near extinction, 'Abdu'l-Bahá, in a talk given on August 28, 1913, spoke of the future of women in society:

In this Revelation of Bahá'u'lláh, the women go neck and neck with the men. In no movement will they be left behind. Their rights with men are equal in degree. They will enter all the administrative branches of politics. They will attain in all such a degree as will be considered the very highest station of the world of humanity and will take part in all affairs. Rest ye assured. Do ye not look upon the present conditions; in the not too distant future the world of women will become all-refulgent and all-glorious, for His Holiness Bahá'u'lláh Hath Willed It So! At the time of elections the right to vote is the inalienable right of women, and the entrance of women into all human departments is an irrefutable and incontrovertible question. No soul can retard or prevent it.

Working Women in American History. Of course, women's suffrage and women's liberation didn't occur overnight. Judith Papachristou, in *Women Together*, outlines a history of women's employment in the United States.[4] In the past, American women did anything and everything to foster the survival of the home. The history of the North and the West especially is peppered with valiant women that held untraditional jobs in order to help their families survive.

By 1900, 20% of the work force were women. Most were still single. The majority regarded work as a stopgap before marriage. Some did continue to work after marriage, but most of these were forced to conceal their marriages in order to preserve their jobs.

Papachristou points out that the middle-class and upper-class girls of the time were encouraged by both the media and the church to believe that their first duties were to the home—caring for the man that God would give them and the children that they were to bear. Women did not have the right to vote, nor did they have any political power in society. They were not admitted to colleges, except to women's colleges, thus their ability to achieve positions of social importance was extremely limited.

Women continued to comprise about 20% of the work force throughout the early part of the twentieth century.

There were fluctuations according to the times. The Depression forced 35% of all women into the work force. This included 9% of all married women. During World War II, the number of married women in the work force rose to 35%. Because of the shortage of men caused by the war, women also moved into traditionally male jobs.

After the war, women were encouraged by the media and the clergy to go back to the home. Contrary to popular belief, however, by the mid-1950s a majority of women were still working outside the home, and almost half were married. In spite of media messages, women have steadily increased in the work force ever since the Depression. By the late 1960s, one third of all female workers were also mothers.[5] According to a recent television special, two-thirds (about nineteen million) of the families in America now have working moms.[6] This means that six out of every ten mothers with children under the age of eighteen are working—38% of these women work full time. This is an increase of 21% from 1970.[7]

The Bahá'í teachings indicate that the mother is the primary educator of her children:

> The task of bringing up a Bahá'í child, as emphasized time and again in Bahá'í Writings, is the chief responsibility of the mother, whose unique privilege is indeed to create in her home such conditions as would be most conducive to both his material and spiritual welfare and advancement. The training which the child first receives through his mother constitutes the strongest foundation for his future development.[8]

On the surface, this appears to present a problem for Bahá'í parents in the United States—especially for the Bahá'í mother. If it is the chief responsibility of the mother to raise the children, and yet women are to enter in all fields of endeavor, how can a woman successfully meet the

challenges of both? Should careers be suspended for children? What if a career cannot be suspended? Are mothers
to continue to work, against their Bahá'í ideals? Or should
Bahá'í mothers only choose careers that can be suspended,
and then resumed once their "chief responsibility" is
completed?

The Universal House of Justice has addressed these concerns. The following is an excerpt from a letter written on
behalf of the House of Justice (dated August 9, 1984) to an
individual believer:

> With regard to your question whether mothers should
> work outside the home, it is helpful to consider the mat-
> ter from the perspective of the concept of a Bahá'í fam-
> ily. The concept is based on the principle that the man
> has primary responsibility for the financial support of the
> family, and the woman is the chief and primary educator
> of the children. This by no means implies that these func-
> tions are inflexibly fixed and cannot be changed and ad-
> justed to suit particular family situations, nor does it
> mean that the place of the woman is confined to the
> home. Rather, while primary responsibility is assigned, it
> is anticipated that fathers would play a significant role in
> the education of the children and women could also be
> breadwinners. As you rightly indicated, 'Abdu'l-Bahá en-
> couraged women to "participate fully and equally in the
> affairs of the world."[9]

The Bahá'í Faith proclaims, as one of its basic tenets,
that women and men are equal. 'Abdu'l-Bahá stressed sexual equality in many of His public talks in Europe and the
United States. He stated that women must engage in all
fields of endeavor, must excel in the arts and the sciences,
and must be responsible for universal peace. Education
is more important for women than education for men.[10]
'Abdu'l-Bahá upheld the importance of women being educated and having the right of the vote. (Women did not

have that right when he visited the United States.) He also praised motherhood, the position that women had held for centuries.

Today's statistics support the statement of 'Abdu'l-Bahá that women would become equal in the world of politics and business. Women have entered the workplace in ever-increasing numbers. Women are breaking ground in new fields every day. There are women in almost every profession—from gas station attendants to executives of major corporations. The movement of women into law, politics, business, arts, and sciences has never before been of such magnitude.

The Current Worldview. Despite all this advancement of women into the business world, the expectations of the society at large are that women are still to remain the primary child rearers. As Marjorie Hansen Shaevitz puts it, this amounts to "yesterday's realities applied today."[11] Our assumptions about motherhood and its duties are still based on the nonemployed-mother stereotype, which is all but passé. The true reality is that the American family is no longer the same as it was even fifteen or twenty years ago. The archetype nuclear family comprises at best only 16% of the population today. Yet, society still maintains the old views of women, and the duties of motherhood. Mothers are expected to serve as they have always served—to give total commitment to hearth and home. They are expected to do most of the parenting, to be able to provide 100% attention to mothering even though they may be holding down a full-time job. According to the editors of *Working Woman*, such unrealistic expectations held by both men and women cause an enormous amount of guilt.[12]

Fathers are reported to want their wives to be more home-minded than career-minded.[13] This expectation was observed by the editors of *Working Woman* when they surveyed attitudes about employed mothers. 54% of the employed men surveyed thought that employed mothers weakened the family. 63% of those men believed that women who wanted a career should not have children. Paradoxically, however, these same men felt that a woman's need for fulfillment through work is just as important as her children's need for the best child care.

With these kinds of attitudes to deal with it is no wonder that women feel guilty. The guilt over whether to work (for those who have already made the choice or who have no choice) is serious. Virtually every study indicates some type of guilt, or "guilty feeling," experienced by mothers.

"Am I doing the right thing?" "Are the children getting enough attention?" Rare is the working mother whose conscience has not been plagued by these questions, whether she is working from necessity or choice, whether the worry is constant or only an occasional intrusion. On the other hand, women still at home think: should I go to work? Would it be fair to my family? How can I work and do everything they need done for them? What will I do after the children are gone?

The brutal fact, however, is that most women don't have a choice when it comes to working. Women and their children represent 75% of the poor in this country. And, 33% of the mothers who work full time are making less than $7,000 a year—far below the poverty line.[14] Nearly two-thirds of all working women are single, widowed, divorced, separated, or have husbands whose incomes are less than $15,000 a year.[15] Most women do not work for the pleasure of a career, but are forced to work in order to survive. The luxury of choosing to work is still reserved, as it has always been, for the upper classes of society.

Despite this, women, and to some degree their husbands, feel guilt about the effect their outside careers have on their children. Francine and T. Douglas Hall suggest that there are two kinds of guilt. The first is the effect one's job may have on being a good parent and on the well-being of the child. The second is guilt about resentment of the child's infringement on one's time, career, or relationship with a spouse.[16] Niki Scott believes that the guilt arises out of men's expectations of women.[17] Shaevitz agrees with this notion but expands it to include all of society and the woman herself.[18]

Speaking as someone who has been a wife and mother, who has worked outside the home, has been a single mother with a career, and most recently has become a full-time housewife/mother, the author has experienced guilt feelings first-hand and from several different angles. Even after confronting them and understanding their origins, she has found guilt still lurking about her subconscious, just waiting to come back to the surface. Surely part of this goes back to a woman's desire to "pull her own weight," to fulfill herself in the world, and at the same time still be a good parent. But society's feeling that homemaking is an archaic occupation, little-praised and under-valued, is part of the problem too.

Twenty-five people were interviewed for this article—ten married couples and five single parents. They overwhelmingly indicated that they felt guilt about leaving their children in the care of others while they worked. Two of the men were single parents with custody of their children. These men spoke about the difficulty of trying to be mother, father, and businessman. The married men commented that they felt less guilt than they thought their working wives did.

One married man admitted that he felt remote from the child-rearing process. He said that his part in fatherhood was a brief moment nine and a half months before the birth of his child. His wife had carried the baby. His wife was the one who bore the child. Even though he participated in the childbirth, he still felt detached. He does have an attachment to his children, but he feels that women, because of their larger part in producing and bearing children, have a greater, more intimate response to the children's needs.

Since the Bahá'í Writings emphasize again and again the primary responsibility of the mother in the rearing of her children, none of this guilt and struggle is misplaced. It is socially and biologically a leaning within each mother and family towards this end. 'Abdu'l-Bahá explains:

> *Furthermore, the education of woman is more necessary and important than that of man, for woman is the trainer of the child from its infancy. If she be defective and imperfect herself, the child will necessarily be deficient; therefore, imperfection of woman implies a condition of imperfection in all of mankind, for it is the mother who rears, nurtures and guides the growth of the child. This is not the function of the father. If the educator be incompetent, the educated will be correspondingly lacking. This is evident and incontrovertible. Could the student be brilliant and accomplished if the teacher is illiterate and ignorant? The mothers are the first educators of mankind; if they be imperfect, alas for the condition and future of the race.[19]*

Mothers and the Workplace. The workplace itself places heavy burdens on parents, and particularly on mothers. The expectations of most employers create conflict for a parent. The parent is expected to take care of the children but not let that interfere with the job.

Many careers, especially the professional ones, require long hours and complete devotion to work with no outside distractions. An employer or client usually cannot be expected to understand that the child was sick all night and that an employee is exhausted from staying up with that child. The same thing holds true for any of the crises of child rearing. For instance, if little Billy falls down at school and breaks his leg, one of the parents must take him to the hospital. Which parent will it be in the case of a two-career couple? Almost universally it will be the mother.

The editors of *Working Woman* say they have found that

the role of psychological parent usually falls onto the woman. Even though men are becoming more involved in home duties, the one that is expected to do all the errands for the children, participate in the PTA, take the children to medical and dental appointments, to dance class, ball practice, and arrange for child care, is still the mother. If that mother has a demanding career (such as lawyer, executive in a large business firm, scientist, or professor at a university), she is faced with the conflict, pressure, stress, and guilt that arises from these expectations of husband, children, society, as well as those from within herself.

Assuaging the Guilt. The Halls believe that dealing with guilt is a matter of coming to terms with one's own expectations and of developing self-confidence to express and meet these expectations. They claim that those who feel less guilty, and can best relieve their stress, are those who are the most comfortable with themselves; those who rely on their own judgement and assertion.

Dr. Matti Greshenfeld asserts that women who work and don't play "martyr" do the best.[19] These are the parents who are more organized and who find ways to get what they feel is most important. They are not afraid to ask for help. They encourage self-reliance in their children. They often have nonessential tasks done by outside help, and they expect help from their spouse (if they have one) in the child-rearing process.

Shaevitz feels that stopping the guilt over child care comes down to adopting one of several contemporary child-rearing models. These models include:

1. *The Sacrificed Career.* Mother or father drops out of the work force to provide full-time care for the children.
2. *Shared Parenting.* Both parents, without depending a great deal on outside help, take care of the children

through flexible work schedules or part-time careers. Parents arrange their own work schedules to meet the needs of the children so that one of them is with the children most of the time.

3. *Substitute Care.* The children are sent to full-time day care, or a full-time housekeeper is hired. This category also includes boarding schools and licensed child-care facilities.

4. *Latch Key.* There is no care at all. The children simply take care of themselves while the parent(s) work. They let themselves into the house and supervise themselves until the adult(s) arrive home.

For Bahá'ís, the secret of dealing with this and other problems rests in the Bahá'í Writings themselves and in applying those precepts to their own lives. Communication is the key to any relationship. Part and parcel of communication is the art of consultation, which is a teaching of the Bahá'í Faith:

The Great Being saith: The heaven of divine wisdom is illumined with the two luminaries of consultation and compassion. Take ye counsel together in all matters, inasmuch as consultation is the lamp of guidance which leadeth the way, and is the bestower of understanding.[20]

Bahá'ís also have the assurance that there is a source of contentment even in the most difficult of times. Being a harried mother, trying to be a breadwinner and a good parent, can produce some of the most difficult tests in a family's life.

If thy daily living become difficult, soon (God) thy Lord will bestow upon thee that which will satisfy thee. Be patient in the time of affliction and trial, endure every difficulty and hardship with a dilated heart, attracted spirit and eloquent tongue in remembrance of the Merciful. Verily this is the life of satisfaction, the spiritual existence, heavenly repose, divine benediction and the celestial table! Soon thy Lord will extenuate thy straitened circumstances even in this world.[21]

In spite of the guilt and the problems of working outside the home, research by Shaevitz indicates that working may in fact be good for the parent—especially the mother. Shaevitz's research shows that working protects women from developing psychiatric symptoms. Work provides self-esteem, meaning to life, and self-control. The nature of the job, according to Shaevitz, has more impact on a mother's well-being and physical health than the fact of working. Relaxed mothers with high prestige jobs tend to fare better than those women who are in jobs that they do not like or that do not afford them high status.

The father also has an impact on the state of the mother. The more support the father gives—whether he lives with the mother or not, the better it is for the woman. The worse the job, and the more inadequate the support for at-home responsibilities, the higher the frustration and insecurity and the more deterioration of the mental and physical health of the parent.

Father's Role. As the roles of women in society and within the family have changed, men have found it especially difficult to accommodate these changes. Since men have continued to hold a view of women as full-time mothers and homemakers, it has been impossible for them to redefine their own social roles. Men still expect to go to work, and to come home to be fed and nurtured by a loving mother and wife.

The reality is that today women are not capable or willing to put out the super-human effort that it would take to mother everyone in the family. Since many women now have careers as demanding as those of their husbands, they need a certain amount of nurturing themselves.

The Bahá'í teachings indicate that the father is expected to take primary responsibility for the economic support of the family and pay for the education of his children. It is also true that the chief responsibility for the early training of the children is that of the mother. But these roles are not rigid. It is anticipated that fathers will play more of a role in child-rearing and mothers will play a greater part in supporting the family. 'Abdu'l-Bahá predicted that there would be more of a balance between masculine and feminine ideals, and less polarization.[22]

Yet, the disparity of expectations between husband and wife often causes tremendous stress within the family. Women can no longer be expected to devote themselves totally to the twenty-four hour nurturance of their families. On the other hand, husbands cannot be expected to assume the role of "nighttime mom" as soon as they arrive home from work. Consultation is needed between husband and wife to arrive at an equitable solution.

The Effects on Our Children. The Halls claim that parenting and careers outside the home are not mutually exclusive. Men have been doing it for years. They state that the old adage of "quality vs. quantity" is valid. Many times, a mother may be home with her children 100% of the time but give them only 20% of her attention or care. Their position is that children benefit from parents working in that they develop a more active part in the responsibility of the family.

Children of working parents tend to cope with problem situations better than those with a full-time parent available in the home. The children of working parents rely less on parents and more on their own resources to solve problems. They appear to be more comfortable moving in and out of social situations and interacting with adults as well as with other children. Research on the question of the quality of the care given to children in day-care centers, housekeeper situations, and full-time parenting has shown that the quality of care depends more on the caregiver than on the facilities where it is given.[22] Smith points out that employed mothers spend only about half the time in direct physical care of their children as do full-time homemakers. However, the husbands of these working mothers tend to spend twice as much time in direct child care as their counterparts with full-time housewives.[23]

Another fact that Smith brings out is that full-time mothers do not spend most of their time stimulating, or affectionately playing with their children. The amount of time spent with the children for both working and at-home mothers depends more upon level of education than on employment status. Ryglewicz and Thaler mention this as well. They list the advantages and disadvantages of parents with outside careers. The list of advantages are:

1. *Lack of mother's attention.* The authors claim that too much attention from mother is harmful for the child's development. They feel it hampers the full development of an independent and self-reliant individual.
2. *The father's role.* The father takes on a more intimate role with children. This produces a more balanced parenting situation for the child. The child learns to appreciate both parents equally.
3. *Quality vs. quantity.* Two-career parents try harder to provide the attention their children need. Therefore even though the amount of time they spend with them is less, the quality of time is enhanced.

On the other side of the coin, according to Rygewicz and Thaler, the drawbacks of working parents are:

1. *Stress.* If the parent(s) are unhappy about working, or frustrated or overstressed, the effect on the children is devastating. The children will most likely feel bad or unloved, as the parent(s) bring home their unhappiness and thus give poor quality time to the children.
2. *Martyrdom complex.* When parents inflict their own guilt on the child by pointing out the sacrifices involved in parenting with an outside career, then the child assumes the guilt for the parent. Too often as children get older, the parent refers to his or her work as the way to provide for all the needs of the child. This can make the child feel that it is his fault that the parent has given up so much to provide for the family. This, of course, can also be true of the full-time parent/caretaker. If the full-time mother continually shows the child that he is her whole life, the child will resent the sacrifice.

Smith points out some other advantages to the children of having parents who have outside careers. He claims that children of working parents tend to be more responsible, do more work around the house, and become more independent as a whole. His research shows that infants of working mothers appear to establish normal attachment relationships. Daughters of working mothers respect their mother more, have less traditional views of marriage and sex roles, and view women as more competent than do daughters of full-time housewives. They are also less likely to devalue the activities of women. Sons of working mothers are more flexible in sex-roles. But once they establish their own homes, they seem to favor the traditional roles (i.e., father as breadwinner, mother as housewife).

The IQ scores and grades of boys of middle-class, working mothers were lower than the boys whose mothers stayed at home. However, girls in the same category seem to do better if the mother worked. Even though IQ scores varied considerably according to the type of day care given, Smith points out that, overall, sons of lower-class employed mothers and daughters of all classes with employed mothers tend to show better academic performance and have higher educational aspirations.

Without doubt, all the research points to the fact that the biggest effect on the children resulted from the attitudes of the parents about their choices. If one or both of the parents resented the mother's involvement in the work force, then the children tended to be more hostile and negative. The stress of the parents was reflected in the children's behavior at school, at home, and in dealings socially.

Day-Care Centers. About 15% of child care provided for youngsters under five years old, is provided in day-care facilities. Only 2% of these facilities are commercial centers such as Kinder-Care, La Petite Academy, or Child's World. The rest range from licensed home-care facilities caring for a handful of kids, to unlicensed housewife-run homes with twenty or more poorly supervised children. Thus generalities arrived at for day-care children are at best an approximation.

The major advantage of day-care centers seems to be that children tend to become more outgoing than their peers raised in the family, or with a full-time parental caretaker. This can also be seen as a disadvantage by some, as day-care children seem to be more boisterous, loud, competitive, and aggressive. However, they are better adjusted when they start kindergarten, more persistent at tasks, and more likely to become leaders.[24] A downside, according to Smith, is that these children also tended to contract more colds, flus, and other contagious diseases.

The quality of the day-care system has been questioned by more than one researcher. Dr. Burton White has criticized the entire system as being unhealthy for the youngsters.[25] He believes that there is no substitute for the total, biased care that a mother or immediate family member can provide. He feels that children under three need that special kind of care and that it cannot be provided in the sterile atmosphere of strangers in a day-care center, or by any caretaker other than immediate family.

Dr. Jerome Kagan disagrees. He feels that parents should be able to find good day-care centers. He believes that two-thirds of the day-care centers are good ones and that there is no ill effect on the children. He feels that the quality of the center can be more easily monitored than that of a home or family-care center where there is little public viewing.

Concerning the issue of nursery or day care, a letter written on behalf of Shoghi Effendi states:

> With reference to the question of the training of children; given the emphasis placed by Bahá'u'lláh and 'Abdu'l-Bahá on the necessity for the parents to train their children while still in their tender age, it would seem preferable that they should receive their first training at home at the hand of the mother, rather than be sent to a nursery. Should circumstances, however, compel a Bahá'í mother to adopt the latter course, there can be no objection.[26]

In any case, most researchers agree that a parent must look carefully at the kind of care their child is receiving while they work. None of the research is old enough to be able to foretell with any certainty the effects that working parents have on their children.

The one concern, voiced by several sources, was the latch-key child. This really amounts to no care at all. Shaevitz regards this as neglect—physical and emotional. But what are parents to do with the children that are too old for babysitters or after-school programs when the demands of the job require the mother to be at work?

We are faced with a society that still believes that the

average mother is home full time to watch over her children, while the reality is not so. The underlying question is how a nation with that assumption can readjust to the reality that most children do not have a full-time parental caretaker. How will we improve our child-care facilities so that parents do not have to worry about their children, and so that there are no children without care?

Fabe and Webler contend that these issues are not private issues but public ones. There is a need for a change in social attitudes and social institutions. The concept of work needs to be reorganized for both men and women, sex roles must be refined (or redefined), and more high quality child care made available. They further state that the United States is far behind other industrialized nations in providing this care. Other nations have made day-care for the young a priority and there are many scheduling options available as well. Such options include, on-premise care at the place of employment, subsidy for day-care provided by employer, state-run or state-sponsored centers, encouragement for better training for the workers at these facilities, flexible hours for both men and women, extended maternity and paternity leave, and so forth.

Presently, in the United States the chief responsibility for the care of children falls upon the shoulders of the parents, and especially the mother. However, there must be support for the growing changes in society. There must be support programs for the children when both parents work and for the single-parent households. Most mothers work outside the home out of necessity and need to have adequate care for their children.

There are many references in the Bahá'í Sacred Writings to the role and importance of motherhood, as well as to the need for women to become involved in all the affairs of the larger society. These two ideals can only be accomplished, however, if the society in which we live accepts the fact that yesterday's values cannot be maintained in today's world. We have outgrown the fantasy of what was. The pressures of modern living and the advancement of women into the business, scientific, and academic arenas require that we take a new look at the problem of child-rearing and at the sex roles of both parents.

Notes

1. United States Bureau of Statistics, 1984.
2. *Monthly Labor Review*. United States Bureau of Labor Statistics.
3. 'Abdu'l-Bahá, *Paris Talks*, pp. 182–84.
4. Papachristou, *Women Together*, pp. 128–32.
5. Ibid., pp. 201–15.
6. "NBC White Paper," Report on Working Mothers, March 16, 1985.
7. Bureau of Labor Statistics.
8. Shoghi Effendi, *Dawn of a New Day*, p. 202.
9. House of Justice, *Women*, pp. 33–34.
10. See numerous references in the public addresses of 'Abdu'l-Bahá found in *Promulgation of Universal Peace, Paris Talks,* and *Star of the West.*
11. Shaevitz, *Superwoman*, p. 79.
12. *Working Woman, The Working Woman Report.*
13. "NBC White Paper."
14. Sarah Weddington, quoted in *San Jose Mercury News*, March 23, 1985.
15. *The Northern California Labor Newsletter.*
16. Hall, Two-Career Couples, pp. 126–48.
17. Scott, *The Working Woman*, pp. 35–50.
18. Shaevitz, *Superwoman*, pp. 79–108.
19. 'Abdu'l-Bahá, *Promulgation of Universal Peace*, pp. 133–34.
20. Bahá'u'lláh, quoted in House of Justice, *Consultation*, p. 3.
21. 'Abdu'l-Bahá, *Tablets of Abdul-Baha*, vol. 1, p. 98.
22. See House of Justice, *Women*, p. 13, no. 25.
23. Smith, *The Subtle Revolution*, pp. 125–52.
24. *Changing Times Magazine.*

25. "NBC White Paper."
26. Written on behalf of Shoghi Effendi to an individual believer, dated July 1940.

Bibliography

'Abdu'l-Bahá. *Paris Talks*. London: Bahá'í Publishing Trust, 1971.

'Abdu'l-Bahá. *Promulgation of Universal Peace*. Wilmette, Ill.: Bahá'í Publishing Trust, 1982.

'Abdu'l-Bahá. *Tablets of Abdul-Baha Abbas*. First published 1909–16. New York: Bahá'í Publishing Committee, 1930.

Brown, Kim. "Do Working Mothers Cheat their Kids?" *Redbook Magazine* (April 1985) vol. clxiv, no. 6.

Changing Times Magazine. "Day Care—Answers for Parents," (August 1984) vol. 38, no. 8.

Fabe, M. and Webler, N. *Up Against the Clock*. New York: Random House, 1979.

Friedan Betty. *The Second Stage*. New York: Summit Books, 1981.

Hall, Francine S. and Douglas T. *The Two Career Couple*. Reading, Mass.: Addison-Wesley Publishing Co., 1979.

Papachristou, Judith. *Women Together: A History of the Women's Movement in the United States*. New York: Alfred A. Knopf, 1976.

Ryglewicz, H. and Thaler, P. K. *Working Couples*. New York: Sovereign Books, 1980.

Scott, N., *The Working Woman: A Handbook*. Kansas City: Sheed Andrews & McMeel, Inc., 1977.

Shaevitz, Marjorie Hansen. *The Superwoman Syndrome*. New York: Warner Books, 1984.

Shoghi Effendi. *Dawn of a New Day, Messages to India 1923–1957*. New Delhi: Bahá'í Publishing Trust, 1973.

Smith, Ralph E. *The Subtle Revolution: Women at Work*. Washington, D.C.: The Urban Institute, 1979.

Toffler, A. *The Third Wave*. New York: Bantam Books, 1980.

Trahey, Jane. *Jane Trahey on Women and Power*. New York: Rawson Associates Publishers, Inc., 1977.

Universal House of Justice. *Consultation: A Compilation.* Wilmette, Ill.: Bahá'í Publishing Trust, 1980.

Universal House of Justice. *Women: Extracts from the Writings of Bahá'u'lláh, 'Abdu'l-Bahá, Shoghi Effendi and the Universal House of Justice.* Thornhill, Ont.: Bahá'í Canada Publications, 1986.

Working Woman Magazine with Gay Bryant. *The Working Woman Report: Succeeding in Business in the 80s.* New York: Simon & Schuster, Inc., 1984.

Working Woman Magazine. The Working Woman Success Book. New York: Hal Productions Inc., 1981.

Depression

by Kathryn Aaron Jaspar

L IKE THE NIGHT, my thoughts were dark. Sitting on a
park bench, lost in a black world of self-deprecation, I
sat fingering the trigger of a loaded gun. At that moment,
the hard metal barrel, cold on my forehead, was my only
real hope. I felt nothing but despair, like a *loser*—unloved,
doomed to failure. There was no love, no joy, no self-
esteem. Nothing.

One part of me wanted desperately to pull the trigger.
Another part of me could not bear the thought of three children growing up to learn that their mother had committed
suicide. *No*, I thought. *I cannot.* Then fear gripped me as I
contemplated returning to everyday responsibilities feeling, as I did, inadequate to be the mother and wife I wanted
to be.

The next day, still alive, I began again the Sisyphean
task of living. It would be years before I learned about the
causes of what has been referred to as the world's number
one public health problem—depression. I only knew then
that the problems in my life were overwhelming. I needed
help; I felt total isolation.

Others who have suffered depression can attest to its
crippling fatigue and accompanying physical illnesses. One

is so drained that there is simply no energy to raise children, to keep house, to love anyone, or to be sufficiently patient to satisfy the emotional needs of others. Depression is a cycle of unending negatives, as if all the cards are stacked against you.

To experience the confusion, the intense guilt, and the hyperemotionalism of depression is to experience fragmentation. It is disorienting. The depressed person needs support, direction, assistance, guidance, and certainly understanding. In my case, neither my husband nor I had any real understanding of the problem, which contributed to further divisiveness. Some days I lived in a fog. At times the frustration was so intense that I would go into the back yard, throw a huge rug over the clothesline, and beat it with a baseball bat. The release helped, but circumstances remained the same.

It was not until ten years later that I was to get medical help for this emotional illness. Recovering from a severe bout with influenza, suffering terrible anxiety and disorientation on my return to the college where I taught, I thought I was going insane. A neuro-psychiatrist prescribed antidepressants for me, and for the first time in my adult life I did not feel suicidal during the holiday season. Compared with previous years, I felt productive, more stable with family, friends, and colleagues. And less fragmented. I was able to experience once again feelings of happiness and well-being. I wondered how I could have felt so lost and inadequate at home and at work.

My doctor explained that the flu virus could have intensified an already present imbalance in brain chemistry: Potent and important substances, called neuro-transmitters, act as messengers that run back and forth across neurons (nerve cells) in order to carry signals from one cell to the next. They deliver a message and then turn off, to wait until a new signal, the *on* impulse, sets them into action again. In depression, when there is a deficiency of the neurotransmitter molecules, the signals are locked into *off*.[1] With the brain locked in off, it cannot receive, store, or transmit messages properly—a malfunction which leaves the person in a dark, negative state, a condition we will see later in destructive cultural patterns. Antidepressants improve the connection between cells, the doctor explained. They help restart the *on* action, so that the brain can register positive emotions of love, joy, and self-esteem. Antidepressants, the doctor said, are to the depressed person what insulin is to the diabetic.[2]

The doctor's explanation began for me an on-going search of over twenty years to better understand the group of symptoms called depressive syndrome.[3] I discovered that anyone could have depression—a writer, a lawyer, an honor student, an actress, a plumber, a housewife and mother, a prime minister, a president—anyone. It appears in those who are stable or neurotic, young or mature, rich or poor. It can be generated from within by internal stress (endogenous) or from outside stress (reactive). Endogenous depression usually has an organic or physical origin, such as the possibly inherited tendency toward manic-depressive disorder. Reactive depression comes, in general, from a sense of loss—from the death of someone close or from a great change in one's life, such as retirement or the time when children leave home.

There is disagreement, however, about the origin of depression associated with social and/or environmental stress due to physical or mental fatigue—the biggest problem facing our society today. Some therapists say destructive thought patterns bring on this type of depression; other experts believe it is caused by an already weakly organized biochemical system taxed with outside stress. In *Up From Depression*, Dr. Leonard Cammer, an eminent psychiatrist, points out that depression resulting from nervous exhaustion emerges from chronic stress—the kind that comes from "the grinding friction of an incompatible marriage, unrelieved slum living, the harshness of an unkind boss, the tyranny of corporate employment, chronic warfare, social turmoil, and so on.'' In these cases of prolonged pressure, he says, acute depression is almost inevitable. It is created by a chemical imbalance in the brain identical with endogenous depression.[4]

If anyone questions the relationship of mental health to stressful conditions, he has only to read *Lives in Stress*, a remarkable study of the feminization of poverty. Many women who once found hope in the women's movement have become disillusioned as a result of their life situations. Having hoped for better jobs and salaries, they find themselves instead often unsupported, as single parents, taxed beyond endurance. Stressed by marital disruptions, inadequate housing, financial strain, large families, and health problems, they succumb to depression. As depressed mothers who have less patience and ability to cope with their families, they communicate these same patterns to their children, and the cycle is continued.[5]

The fact is that in depression one is cut off from positive emotions: from the soul, from joy, from the very essence of life. The mind is locked into a vicious cycle. Depression triggers negativity which, in turn, triggers more severe depression. The body does not want to function. One wonders which comes first—the chicken or the egg? The negative feelings or the chemical imbalance? As one sees the increasing number of attempted suicides in our country, indeed in the world, and sees the growing number of men and women seeking help with their poor self-images, it is natural to wonder where all this bad stuff is coming from.

It is estimated that eight to twelve million Americans are suffering from depression; over fifteen million may need some treatment.[6] Although it is considered the common cold of psychiatric disturbances, depression is a devastating cycle of negative thinking which can be life threatening. Every sufferer is a candidate for suicide.

What is going on in a society where suicide is the second leading cause of death among adolescents and college students, and the tenth leading cause of all deaths? Where an estimated 200,000 to 500,000 people a year try to kill themselves?[7] Where women, and men, by the hundreds of thousands more have low self-esteem? Where pent-up anger turns outward into violence, or inward into guilt, frustration, and depression? Only by the eclectic approach, gathering from all fields, can we begin to see the whole of this very complex phenomenon which has come to be the *most common emotional problem of Western culture.*[8]

What Is Depression? Depression, like a Shakespearean drama, can be viewed on many levels: There is the physical aspect, the emotional struggle and, the ethical, spiritual battle. All of these levels interrelate. And, inevitably in a Bahá'í's search to define the boundaries of responsibility and freedom, some probing questions arise: Is it a physical, mental, or spiritual problem? Is it something I bring on myself because I am not spiritual enough? Is it genetic and therefore basically physical? Is it a test from God? Does it have to do with environment and stress, or—with socialization in our roles as children and parents? When do I stop being radiant and acquiescent to others' demands and start to demand justice for myself? Is my religious zeal manic?

Farzaneh Guillebeaux, a Bahá'í and a marriage and family therapist in Montgomery, Alabama, explains that a first step in overcoming depression may be to explore inner fear.[9] We have negative self-images that we have accepted as reality. And when our cultural conditioning is based on destructive negative social concepts, it can erode self-confidence and bring about depressive thoughts that prevent our mental and spiritual growth; it can obscure the radiant reality of our latent talents and spiritual attributes.

Know Thyself. In every revealed religion we find the mandate to know ourselves, know our own essence. There is no other situation where this principle is more valuable than in depression. It is imperative to be aware of one's inner strengths as well as weaknesses: one's tendency to distort reality by under-valuing a situation in depression, or over-valuing it in mania. As Bahá'ís, we are clearly told that our essence is the same as the essence of God, that our talents and latent nobility await discovery. The gifts or talents bestowed upon us, hidden within the spirit in our souls, are rejected if we do not seek to know and to develop them. We each have unlimited capacity for growth in nobility, insight, love, might, truthfulness, justice, openness, creativity, and so on. When we lose sight of this concept, Guillebeaux points out, we get into trouble. One form of that trouble is depression. We become depressed and fearful of knowing ourselves. Why?

Part of the test of depression is to find the answer. We must take the responsibility to get help—whether by introspection, by medical means, by counseling, and/or by therapy—to follow the greatest mandate, to know ourselves. When Bahá'u'lláh tells us to look within ourselves and to find Him standing there, He gives us a hard task. For we live in a devastating age which has thrown confusing images onto our mental screens from literature, from television, from the material world. We see only fragments. Are we sexual objects? Are we objects of material consumption, as advertising would have us believe? How do we choose our image? We must try to see through the error of our social conditioning to find out how we can utilize the bounty of the Faith as our lifeline.

Learned Helplessness. One reason for the poor self-image that many women and men carry within themselves almost certainly lies in the cultural roots of learned helplessness. Of course, most of us do not realize this until we find ourselves caught in the role of the helpless, submissive partner associated with depression—wondering why we work so hard for the spouse-approval or parent-approval which never seems forthcoming. One explanation of this underlying paradox may lie in the conflicting values of men and women regarding the goal of human development. As women seek male approval and do not receive it, they feel helpless. One reason for the lack of approval by men is that men value independence and autonomy as a goal, whereas women value bonding more highly.[10]

The woman realizes that her natural tendencies are culturally undervalued, so she submits to the male principle of autonomy. It is almost as if her natural concern for bonding is used to her disadvantage. As a result, she often enters a dominant-male and passive-dependent-female relationship, where the male is authoritarian and demanding, while the female is encouraged to be sacrificial and helpless.[11] Because girls in our society are taught to respect masculine values, and the boys are brought up to devalue femininity, they both learn to consider self-assertion and competence in women as unattractive.[12] Yet in Western culture it is hammered home that women need approval.[13]

In my own case, I felt subjected to constant criticism from my husband. Despite the fact that we were both equally educated and working at equally creative and well-paying jobs, I was fearful of his frequent emotional outbursts. As a result, I adopted a submissive stance to ensure peace and unity in the family. There were times, after the fact, that I realized this approach was destructive—for example, when one of my sons might be punished unjustly, or when I complied with my husband's wishes by not assisting my sons and daughter financially in college (something which I felt strongly about) because he wanted them to make it on their own. I am now convinced that my reticence was more destructive than if I had spoken out and demanded my fair voice, but that was how I kept peace in the family at the time. It is often difficult indeed to decide which is best—to demand justice and risk divisiveness or to capitulate in order to maintain family unity.

Eventually I took a stand, but not until I realized it is impossible to make another person happy by submitting to his demands. In those earlier years of marriage, other questions I might have asked myself were: "What about family unity including the feelings of the co-provider?" and, "Although you may fear the stigma of divorce, would the children be better off away from this situation?" Eventually, I came to see that, through an accumulation of trivial incidents, power in our home had been handed over almost exclusively to my husband because of his ability to rationalize his points and to convince me that I was emotional and irrational. When I worked late in my office at the college where I taught, for example, I would get the blame for his irritation and suspicion; it seemed hopeless to explain that I could work better there, where it was quiet and there was less confusion.

The Bahá'í writer Marzieh Gail, in *Dawn Over Mount Hira*,[14] talks about the tensions of transition that women have undergone in their struggle to become equal participants in marriage and careers. Traumatic wounds are inflicted in this struggle, she says, that often leave the children with lifelong psychic damage. It seems to me this was true for my own family. As a woman I knew I was essential in the role of establishing spiritual values and non-prejudicial policies in the home, on the one hand, but that I had to stifle my opinions in order to maintain unity, on the other. This kind of tension adds to a woman's fragmentation of feelings, thoughts, and behavior, and to the children's confusion.

Dr. Natalie Shainess, a prominent New York psychiatrist and psychoanalyst, author of *Sweet Suffering: Woman as Victim*, refers to this hopelessness/helplessness role as a form of unconscious masochistic behavior which is learned during childhood. In this behavior, the person—feeling worthless and afraid of offending—often apologizes when it is not necessary, shrugs off compliments, agrees with others merely to avoid conflict, feels guilty when she says no to requests for favors, and postpones asking for something she wants or needs.[15] Taken to the extreme, this self-effacing behavior can jeopardize personal safety. Alone at night and walking to her car, rather than risk his displeasure, a woman may stop to answer an unknown man's question, an act which gives him the edge in an attack. She does this rather than follow her inner instincts to refuse him.

This woman's role as a spouse is one of submissiveness, one in which she has a morbid interest in *things*, and longs for her husband's assertiveness, a quality which she has neither opportunity nor cultural encouragement to express. Because of her unhealthy, self-deprecating manner, she is willing to serve her partner in an *I'm nothing, he's everything* relationship.[16] And yet, despite her servile role, the man persists in his contempt for her behavior.

In *Me, Myself and I*, Bahá'í author and therapist, Dr. Ann Schoonmaker calls this relationship a spell of romantic love, as the woman obtains her identity from the husband in what is referred to as a Cinderella relationship.[17] As the spell continues, the partners hold each other back from the social and spiritual growth that is the natural outgrowth of loving consultation between respectful, equal partners. Instead of approaching serious issues as problems subject to rational and spiritual solutions, the wife holds back for fear of possible hostility, while the husband fails to see the need for consultation on a question he considers solved unilaterally in his own mind.

Masochistic, submissive patterns begin at an early age, Shainess says, when conflict between the parent's needs and those of her child emerge. The mother may not realize that she resents her child's demands, yet in subtle ways she punishes the child by delaying feeding and touching, or by showing anger. Thus, at an early age the child senses disapproval. Later, verbal abuse is added to other negative conditioning. When the child asks why the angry parent is angry, she is told, "I'm not angry with you; I love you." Rather than fulfilling the child's needs, the adult fosters self-doubt in the child until the child's image of herself, and her belief in her own badness, becomes grounding for future feelings of worthlessness, guilt, and helplessness—all associated with depression.[18]

Anger. Closely related to notions of poor self-image due to learned helplessness is the theory that anger turned inward can cause depression. Although some authorities feel there is little empirical evidence to support the anger/depression theory, it is worthwhile to examine the idea. In their book, *The Book of Hope: How Women Can Overcome Depression*, Dr. Helen De Rosis and Victoria Pellegrino reinforce Dr. Shainess' masochistic behavior theory.[19] They ascribe the major root of depression to frustration developed as a result of trying to please everyone. A woman becomes angry about the dilemma in which she finds herself. She feels guilty about the anger, and then attempts to squelch her anxiety by avoiding her feelings. She may turn those feelings inward. Finally, the victim turns off all her feelings as a defensive move. Deadness is the core of all depression, they say.[20] This deadness leads to fatigue and inertia, symptoms that rob a woman of creativity and initiative. Eventually, because of conflict within herself, she becomes indecisive. De Rosis and Pellegrino make it clear that potential help exists in rethinking culturally rooted anxieties, changing one's distorted view when locked into depression.

There are other powerful examples to be found in our society of anger turned inward. One is the woman who finds herself at home suffering through the role of lost motherhood. She undergoes both a painful decline of self-esteem and feelings of being cheated out of life's rewards, but she is unable to admit anger toward the children who are no longer responsive.[21] At the same time she makes rigid demands on herself and finds it hard to expand her interest to new areas of occupation and community activities. One woman continued to rank helping her children as her most important role during a mid-life crisis, but then added that they no longer needed her.[22]

It is not only women who get into trouble as a result of not expressing their feelings; there are equally destructive social patterns that bring about noncommunicative, nonexpressive attitudes in men.[23] And, while it is reported that more women are depressed than men, it may well be that men do not seek help because of their social conditioning.

Marriage and family therapist Guillebeaux points out that, although boys receive more positive praise and encouragement than girls, they also receive more pressure to avoid behavior inappropriate for their sex and have less value placed on excellence in creative areas.[24] In the father role, the male may have the posture of calculated aloofness, of avoidance, in the home environment, whereas the mother is the nurturer. These two opposing attitudes seem to lock the male child into a position of accepting emotional nurturance on the one side, and yet of rejecting his own nurturing feelings as he matures. Furthermore, whereas girls are taught to act gently, boys learn to devalue qualities of gentleness and responsiveness and to value competition, aggressiveness, and action. What parents communicate by these attitudes is that a man cannot be an affectionate, tender, communicative person.[25]

The price to be paid for the rigidity of male socialization is a life-and-death matter. Because he cannot express feelings and must keep emotions bottled up, and because he is pressured to be successful, to accomplish, to provide— all qualities of achieving, rather than of being open and communicative, the price is a higher mortality rate either through depression and suicide, or by fatal stress diseases such as alcoholism. Research shows that psychological factors contribute even more to higher mortality than genetic factors.[26] Gloria Steinem observed this point in a 1970

Time article where she reported that men suffer from more diseases due to stress, such as heart attacks and suicide, a situation now increasingly noted in women subject to the same career stresses.[27]

When a man reevaluates his role in the family and his home-oriented tasks, he risks embarrassment at times, something he avoided in the past. He also risks being considered feminine in the new nurturing role, a role that might have been considered emasculating in the past.[28] As men increase their involvement with home-oriented tasks, shifting from the stereotypically masculine role, they may experience some anxiety and ambivalence. But those fathers and husbands who make the transition have also voiced positive feelings about showing their children ways to ask for help, and about getting away from the macho habits of telling boys to be strong, not to cry, etc.[29]

Assertiveness. Within my own experience, I first thought that my depression was basically due to an inherited tendency toward a biochemical imbalance triggered by severe viral infection, as my doctor explained. It did not occur to me that it had anything to do with my upbringing or my marriage. But as I have progressed through a number of severe episodes, wondering again and again which came first —the chemical imbalance or the despair and negative feelings—I have become aware of how not being assertive in my early years of marriage and child-rearing may have contributed to depression.

Not to be assertive meant a kind of self-destruction at certain times: When I had the opportunity for a sabbatical leave, under pressure at home, I chose the half-year sabbatical at full pay, rather than a less hectic full year at half pay. I thus placed myself under greater stress to complete the work required during this shorter time of study. Had I simply insisted on the full year, which was what I needed, no doubt we would have worked it out. He surely would have chosen that had our roles been reversed. But because social conditioning and depression robbed me of feelings of self-worth, I was passive and gave in. It seems to me now that much of this conditioning is a result of our society's orientation that to be good is to sacrifice, especially for a woman. The perspective of our present Dispensation is more clearly based on the principle that to be good is to be *just* also. The trick is to decide when to give in to others, and when to be just and assertive. We fool ourselves if we direct our energy toward making others happy, toward controlling others' lives to make ourselves feel more secure. As a Bahá'í, I have learned to value being just, although our society in general does not support such behavior in women, especially within the family.

To ignore the inner self is to bring about an emotional and spiritual deadness. We are fragmented when we do not assert ourselves and are forced to stuff our feelings away somewhere, unexamined, because of custom or pressure from a stressful environment. Feelings become separated from thoughts. Then, with no outlet for anger, the powers of such emotions may burst forth in a violent, irrational direction of their own. This kind of response often happens in depression, during a time when a person has little control over emotional reactions. On the other hand, when we take charge of these emotions and allow them to surface in order to deal with them, we free up our thinking.

Of course, not all feelings will be spiritual ones of righteous indignation. A person may think, "Oh, the children are disturbing the Feast," or "Oh, I hate sitting in Assembly meetings." But to express this truthfully and consult with someone about it becomes a creative challenge. One therapist, for example, suggested to someone in the latter situation that he attend only one hour (or only one half) of the next Assembly meeting and then reevaluate his capacity for future meetings. Bahá'ís are free to be creative in problem-solving. Rigidity brings about frustration, depression. Letting go of rigid demands placed on ourselves, obsessively at times, can be painful. But with help, we discover significant feelings we were previously unaware of, because we were so focused on control. When there is an inner congruence, an inner unity of thoughts and feelings and behavior, when nothing is held back or repressed, then there is integration of all components of our individuality, what we might call mental health.[30] In a Bahá'í context, we are reflecting our essence, the essence of God. In other words, we are taking responsibility for thoughts and feelings that are not wholly conscious as well as for our conscious ones. A totally aware person does not say to others: "I am a Bahá'í," and then, while assuming a Bahá'í role, go off and act some other way, pretending not to notice his own mistakes. What we can do, though, is to say: "I will do this much Bahá'í today," a statement which confirms our spiritual essence while at the same time acknowledging our limitations.[31]

It would be unwise, however, to consider assertiveness the only solution to helplessness. Sometimes the right action may be to do nothing, or to cooperate for the sake of unity. Dr. Arnold P. Nerenberg reminds us in his sensitive book, *Love and Estrangement in the Bahá'í Community*, that each day at noon we acknowledge our powerlessness in relation to God's might so that when we see powerlessness in others, we can feel compassion.[32] Powerlessness is something we can each identify with. Bahá'í women may have a doubly difficult time learning ways of handling helplessness and submissiveness, for we know we are equal and should assert our rights, and yet we know all Bahá'ís are taught in the Writings to be loving and cooperative, indeed —to sacrifice for one another. It is the balance, then, between these two things—assertiveness and sacrifice— which we must obtain.

My River Odyssey. At one time in my teaching career, I became so ill I could no longer work. It was hard to comprehend how I had come to such a state. It seemed to me that everything in my life was working against me: My children had all left home, either to get married or to attend college; my husband and I had separated for the second time; and now my profession, a source of satisfaction and self-esteem for almost twenty years, was threatened because of poor health. I questioned the very meaning of life.

I do not know how one goes in search of meaning. For me, it has always been through experience that I have come to understandings. The same was to hold true for the most important event of my life, a river journey on the Mississippi at a time when I felt living held no promise, when I felt only fear that I would shrivel up, yet continue to exist —like a paralyzed, catatonic patient who has no will to go in any direction.

I decided on the Mississippi River trek, and the crossing to the Florida Keys, after months of severe depression accompanied by a debilitating physical illness, and months of psychotherapy, recommended by a local Spiritual Assembly to help in resolving an inner conflict. I had lost weight; I had no energy. But I fantasized about the luxury of sea, sky, and weather that might make people in St. Louis envious as they hustled in the sleet, lungs stinging from frost. Although my husband, Dennis, and I were separated, and were in the midst of making decisions about our marriage, our property, our future, he talked about leaving his job with the government and taking his thirty-five-foot sailboat down the river to the Florida Keys. I could either go, he said, or retire from life and give up. For Dennis, the trip would be the first leg of a journey to England to see his mother. I could go as far as Florida and stay there awhile, or continue on.

On unconscious levels I longed for the salt air, squawking cries of gulls, cumulus clouds sculptured against blue, sunlit skies. These drew me to the eternal surging beauty of the sea, to the source of life, to the *cradle endlessly rocking.* Further, the trip would be an experiment which might bring us together to resolve our differences. I decided I wanted to be there. I had almost no alternative.

Whenever I think back over the months of that trip, recalling the outer and inner changes of my life, I am always grateful to Dennis for the experience which returned to me a sense of aliveness and—by the end of the journey—direction. What brought about these changes in physical strength and regained confidence? What was it that came from one thing and flowed into another? Where does the body stop and the mind start? And the spirit? In *Gleanings*, for example, we are told by Bahá'u'lláh that the energy required for performing the functions of sight, hearing—all our senses—is dependent upon the rational faculty of the soul.[33] And that if we were to ponder *"from now until the end that hath no end,"* we would not be able to comprehend the mystery of the soul.[34] It must have been the interaction of all components of the individual which worked together for an effect. I began to see everything in a new way; as if by magic I had been invited from the darkness of a theater, as an observer caught in conflicting roles of mother, Bahá'í, wife, teacher, to step onto a lighted stage to play a fresh, new role. Each day was unique, not routine. And there was so much beauty.

The events on board the ocean-going sloop *Nashallah* unfolded in a very different way from what we had anticipated. What was to have been two weeks on the river became five, long, cold weeks, followed by a freezing spell in dry-dock on the gulf coast, climaxed by two gulf crossings on a dark, rough sea. The only crew member, our son-in-law Horst Rietschel, suffered an arm injury on the winch when *Nashallah* ran aground near Memphis; he had to return home. I was then forced to play the role of what might euphemistically be called the "crew." In the Middle East, when they make plans, they say, *Insha'llah!* (if God wills).

In the early planning stages, I had thought it best for me

to fly to New Orleans, forgoing the Mississippi passage. But I could not bypass the stretch of river that had lured Huck Finn for nearly twelve hundred miles. It is easy to see why Mark Twain used the river as a powerful symbol in *Huckleberry Finn*, for it is god-like in its primordial force. The widest sections can appear quiet and silvery, as sun-sparkling rivulets play across the water onto sandy beaches. But the river may suddenly become shallow enough to leave a boat stranded in front of an on-coming barge. Or, in deeper water there may be whirlpools that make control of a vessel almost impossible. In some areas, the channel is so narrow, and depth so critical, that going off course for only moments could be disastrous.

It took only a few days on the river for us to set up a routine, to establish a rhythm. Each day I woke to the gentle rocking motion of the boat and the churning of the engine. Because I felt so awfully bad in the mornings, I rested in my bunk in the aft cabin while the men made coffee and started the forty horsepower Pices engine before beginning the day's trek downriver. Later, I prepared a hot breakfast in the L-shaped galley and rested until noon. It seemed like only minutes until three in the afternoon, when we had to find a safe anchorage, navigate to the spot, and set anchor before dusk; otherwise we ended up setting anchor at nightfall, unsure of the ground and currents. The evening ritual gave a sense of familiar comfort as we lit the kerosene lamps before supper. Then our world, which had been so endless in daylight, narrowed to our sturdy vessel of finely crafted teakwood and white fiberglass. Designed by naval architect Bruce Bingham and built in one of the most respected Taiwanese shipyards, the model known as the *Fantasia* combined oriental beauty with the solid structure of a wide berth and a four-ton keel. But no matter how sturdily built a vessel, when moored, it is only as safe as its anchor.

Anchoring at dark is dangerous and challenging, but it brings with it a deep appreciation for life that is missing in the seemingly safe city. When the wind picks up and is whistling through the halyards, the boat bucking on the anchor as the current rushes noisily past, you want to know you can put your head on the pillow and wake up in the same spot, that you will not be sliding out into the main channel to be wiped out by a barge. After a few nights like that, you soon learn to appreciate a calm one.

Whereas anchoring is the key to survival at night, navigation is everything during daylight. Someone must be on constant lookout for each nun or can marking the main channel, so the helmsman can maintain proper depth for safe passage. In sunny weather, it is pleasant to sit in the mid-cockpit or stand on deck to keep watch, but only a few days out of St. Louis, the cold northers began; we had cold, damp, and finally, sleet to contend with. On our boat, Horst was the best lookout, as he watched with binoculars for the buoys and pointed them out to the helmsman.

Taking the helm is serious business. When the weather turned cold on the first leg downriver, I relieved the men so they could warm themselves in the main cabin on their lunch break. I found it could be confusing at the helm—the red and black buoys, the radio contact with barges, the binoculars, the instructions from barge captains—all at one time. Even so, I managed.

Peering through the binoculars, I would catch the dot of a distant marker. Red nun, so stay to the right. Ah, there's an approaching barge silhouetted on the horizon. Juggling the helm and the binoculars, I would switch to the VHF radio frequency used to speak directly to barges.

"This is the southbound pleasurecraft sailboat *Nashallah* to the northbound barge at Hardscrabble Bend (or whatever landmark was near). Which side do you want us on, skipper?"

"Well, either's all right. Slide by on two whistles. I'll ease out."

For a second or two, I would think again which side the

barge captain meant. Two whistles, pass him on his right; one whistle is left. Then I would make the proper adjustment at the helm and confirm instructions.

"Roger, skipper; on the two whistles. Thanks, 'n have a good trip."

"OK, 'n you all have a good one goin' down," he would answer.

After steering past the barge, I would veer away from the wake. If the tow was tearing along, the wake was tremendous, like huge waves in the sea, and *Nashallah* pitched like a bronco. It gave me confidence to handle her.

As the outer voyage took on significance, it was not long before I discovered that something was happening within me. Something within the depths of my depression, here on this boat, was changing. I was beginning to feel a new sense of aliveness. My body felt tired at the end of a long day; a gurgling from my stomach signaled lunchtime. There was excitement in weighing anchor in the misty mornings. Stark fear in danger. These feelings—tired, hungry, happy, fearful—seemed to reawaken dormant energies. Grounded in activities aboard *Nashallah*, my life, and the rhythm of the river, began to take on meaning. I no longer was going in three or four directions at once, or in no direction at all.

Living aboard *Nashallah*, I realized that I had been living in a state of deprivation. Was it from eating on the run? driving on the Interstates? pushing aside signals for help from within, as a victim of numbness who no longer felt the need to survive? As a Bahá'í I was supposed to help others with projects, grieve with others, but how could I respond to anyone when functioning at such a frenetic pace? There was stress on the river. But, somehow it was different. Unlike driving on the expressway unaware of real danger, the river odyssey was in the midst of danger, where it could be faced and accepted as reality. Here, in the cul-de-sac of a boat, I perceived awakening in me a physical appreciation for life that had been missing in suburbia. Closer to the elements in nature, we felt the sunshine and air when the hatch stayed open. Even in the rain and cold, it was necessary to stick my head outside to see what was happening.

Whereas on land one may need continual stimulation to maintain interest in life, on a boat one has placed himself at the mercy of the elements and his own inventiveness. The requirements of pleasure are lowered: food, once a gourmet's delight, becomes a study in nourishment. There are no McDonald's burger places to stop at once you leave the St. Louis arch. A simple bowl of hot soup becomes a luxury beyond words, after being on watch in icy wind. I now found myself, like a farm wife cooking for hired hands, preparing stews with lentils or thick split-pea soup with plenty of onions and carrots for the men to stay nourished until anchoring at dusk. On the other hand, I often collapsed, after making that lunch, while my body was ferried along the river, like Cleopatra reclining on the Nile.

One soon learns to appreciate such simple things as water, electricity, and kerosene—commodities easily taken for granted in the suburbs, but found in limited supply on a boat. I learned to rinse each cup and dish with only a few drops of water. When the diesel chugged along, I loved the hot water for cooking and cleaning. For coffee and meals like stew, made on a gimbaled propane stove, I did not use one minute's worth of propane without planning what to use it for, so that no gas was wasted. We all treasured the small, Aladdin kerosene stove-heater that Dennis bought. This marvel sat well balanced in the middle of the main salon. Standing only two feet high, its blue flame hissed quietly day in and day out as it kept the temperature inside comfortable. Important too, the kerosene lamps lit each evening at dusk. They saved battery-powered electric lights on board. And, more importantly, they gave a glow that reflected off of the carved teakwood bulkheads and magically changed the world of approaching darkness into one of old-world warmth and beauty.

After Horst injured his arm, my role took on added significance. Although he had been certain that his arm was not broken, at Memphis we got the news that, in fact, it was. When the winch handle slips with a weight of two thousand pounds on the line, one could hardly expect otherwise. We had no way of knowing then the months of anguish he would suffer because of the injury, but we were saddened by his leave-taking and felt his presence for a long while. With Horst gone, I had longer spells at the helm than before, and also assisted with setting and weighing anchor. Fortunately, we had radio contact with another craft, the *Kookaburra*, the 26-foot cabin cruiser home of two young men from Travers City. At night we anchored near each other and rafted up to share tea and impressions of the day, to celebrate the coming of evening, with its iridescent reflections of Renoir blues and pinks. As I grew stronger, I became more active; in Baton Rouge my strength was put to a real challenge because of a new element of alarm: freighters. With no dockage for pleasure craft, we tied up at a portable fueling barge equipped with three gasoline pumps and a crew in bright orange vests. When the tri-fueller traveled at night, we moved our boat to a spot next to the *Kook*, where other boats jumped and churned from the turbulent wake produced by in-coming and out-going freighters. One night we stood on the wharf and literally held our vessels apart so as not to strike one another. I considered myself very important in keeping *Nashallah* from damage.

As the rhythmic flow of each day down river continued, I began to feel more like my old self of several years before, strong and self-confident. Then, before New Orleans, we holed up for several days at Profit Island Chute, a protected side of an island, because of mist and fog. It was beautiful there, with a lovely, long sandbar to protect us from barges ploughing along, and we had rest and time to meditate. As the morning mist rose above the sandbar, white heron and ibis stalked leisurely along the shore water, zapping unseen delights with their beaks.

Basking in such beauty, I felt a sudden release of energy; I realized that I wanted more than anything to do something creative; to do things I had ached to do while teaching: to read, to do some writing, but most of all to watercolor and paint, to get into art. I knew then that the part of myself with which I had lost touch was the creative person. But that was not all I was to discover. That evening Ken and John rowed over from the *Kook* in their dinghy with dinner, sweet, rich spaghetti that Ken had prepared from a special recipe. As we sat in our oil-lit world, the lamplight bouncing off our faces and the teakwood surrounding us, John asked me how I liked living aboard as a life-style. Sputtering out that it was "great," I faked the answer. Truthfully, I was horrified at the ambivalence within me revealed by his question. I loved being on the boat, but I was experiencing an increasing urgency for time alone not possible there. I couldn't say that I had, just that very day, been thinking about how much I wanted my own direction apart from Dennis. Can't anything be simple, I wondered.

My conflict had nothing to do with caring for Dennis, for, despite many family difficulties, we cared about one another and about helping each other. Confident of his ability to handle any emergency aboard *Nashallah*, I admired his competence as captain; furthermore, the division of responsibility resolved any conflict regarding our respective roles. Without the river trip, I would not be regaining my health and interest in life. Still, I found myself wondering if we were not more partners sharing an experience on this magnificent river than partners in marriage. There was the river odyssey, and there was the relationship between us—they were turning out to be separate. I decided that I would discuss all this with Dennis when we got to New Orleans.

Although we entered the city at night in mid-December, it was like the Fourth of July. Lights everywhere! Lighted silhouettes of freighters docked at industrial sites reflected on the water. Lights on all boats moving or stationary, skyscrapers, anchored freighters, all threw brilliant multi-colored patterns on the river. It seemed a warm welcome after twelve hundred miles down the Mississippi. The next day, after finally navigating through the industrial canal, with numerous locks and bridges, to the entrance of Lake Pontchartrain, what a glorious sight to find balmy winds! Blossoming flowers in flashing reds and yellows, clouds drifting lazily against the Caribbean blue sky. I felt happy about our achievement.

Before we left to cross Pontchartrain to the ocean to our first sail, I shared my deepest thoughts with Dennis. It was very difficult, but a relief to both of us to talk. Neither of us spoke up to say we wanted to be married. Dennis was be-coming involved with the boat community there, and he spent many evenings with friends talking over cruising and charts. I became more fully aware that I wanted to leave af-ter we arrived in Florida. I decided that, before finalizing my decision, I would fly back to St. Louis for some counsel-ing both in psychotherapy and with the local Spiritual As-sembly. Making the decision was painful. I could hardly stand the thought, and yet it was exciting as well. As I al-lowed my feelings to surface, there seemed to be a sense of integration, a regenerating insight: as if, like putting to-gether one of those children's puzzles with large pieces of the body, I was putting into place—one at a time—the sec-tions of the head, the heart, and the body so that the parts fit together as one whole person.

Confronting these feelings frightened me. The most ter-rible part was having to admit to myself that I had not been truthful about my motives for coming on the boat. It was not that I had lied consciously, I realized, but that I had used the boat trip as an excuse to get to the ocean, to get somewhere to touch the essence of what had been placed within me by the One. I had only pretended that the trip would resolve all the differences between my husband and me. Part of my conflict had been that I was split between trying to make myself do what I felt I had to do as a mother, wife, teacher, Bahá'í, and listening to powerful inner feelings that signaled a different direction. I wanted to follow my desires to go on the boat, but I had to disguise them in a Bahá'í covering. Besides fooling others, I had fooled myself. I kept thinking how ironic it was that we had named the boat *Nashallah, If God Wills.* I had been so convinced that the boat would be our chance to work things out that I had voted for that name over several others. I felt confident, however, in my growing decision; at the same time I valued the years of my life with Dennis and our experience aboard *Nashallah.* I also felt confident that he would find another mate (as he eventually did) who would be more boat-oriented, with whom to share his life.

We had good winds on the gulf on the first sail, and *Nashallah* heeled like a veteran ocean-going vessel. The weather, a burst of blue sky and sunshine, was the kind one dreams about up on the chilly section of the Mississippi called Alton Lake, near St. Louis. My excitement was boundless as the sails exploded in the gulf wind. I took the helm of a real boat in a real ocean. I could hardly wait to tie up at Gulf Port where friends had dinner waiting for us: I was anxious to discuss the first sail with Dennis, to share the declaration of our accomplishment, our risk-taking.

But we never talked. After a lovely dinner, the men sat up late into the night talking charts and cruises. Returning to my bunk, I collapsed exhausted, feeling cheated and disappointed. No matter what our relationship, I deserved better. I felt humiliated. He preferred talk about the passage and sail with his boating pals than with the wife who had shared his achievement.

Before making any final decisions about my life, I flew to St. Louis for counseling while we had the *Nashallah* in dry dock in Gulf Port. When I returned to the boat and confirmed my plan to leave after we reached Florida, Dennis remained dejected for days. But I observed an underlying sense of relief; he had not been forced to make any decisions. More secure for the first time in years, I felt integrated, solidified. The river returned to me my goals, my direction. An escape from city pressures of phones, schedules, highways, the river passage offered lessons in camaraderie, simplification of life, and oneness with nature. I was learning how to pace myself better, how to avoid rigidity in roles. At times, in fact, I felt a little like a chameleon; I played a variety of roles—crew member, wife, partner on board, writer, artist. On the first long crossing to Tarpon Springs I had an experience that reinforced my newly found awareness, a unique and memorable event during my first time alone at the helm, in open water on a pitch black night, without a sliver of a moon.

Harboring an irrational fear that some uncharted obstruction would loom up in front of me, and worried about holding course in a rough, following sea, I found myself dwelling on all the many changes in my life since leaving home and, once again, asking myself if everything was settled. I could see absolutely nothing in the unknown blackness. Out of nowhere came rushing, blowing sounds loud enough to be whales. From the faint glow of the running lights, I could see forms, white, like bodies of nude women swimming in the night sea, undulating, porpoising about, diving, blowing. As they ran alongside us, these captivating dolphins, passing under the bow, sporting like clowns in the perfection of their element, one female rolled sideways, her eye open to gain a direct view of me. As our eyes met, I sensed her glance, inquisitive—as if in looking into another world, she wondered what we were doing there, yet sympathetic at the same time. That look was wonderful. I felt honored to have the dolphins with us. Out of the terrifying darkness came these numinous forms, moving spirit-like across the water. I had an overpowering sense of their presence, not unlike sea-nymphs guiding Ulysses on his fearful voyage. Though the elements around me remained the same, their lightening effect seemed like a mystical sign of confirmation.

There were other crises and challenges that accompanied the beauty of my river passage. When I think back on some of them, my mind becomes a kaleidoscopic whirl of memories: a magenta sunset at New Madrid, our last stop with Horst before Memphis; the noise of hooting freighters clipping by in the night; the surreal blending of sky and water into a curtain of iridescent blues and pinks; the warmth of the Christmas meal Dennis and I shared with friends ensconced aboard the *Nashallah*, a poinsettia presented to us for a tree, winds whistling above; the fuchsia-topped Coast Guard station at West End at Pontchartrain; the journey within, the awakening of skills that offered meaning and a new sense of being alive. An acceptance of life.

The path to acceptance of life can be painful. Despite all the good that came from the river journey, the exercise and better health, the resolution of inner conflict, and the regained confidence, there were times I felt waves of anxiety flood over me. When the boat was in dry dock on the gulf coast, I walked, in anguish, down a road near the harbor, wringing my hands and practically tearing my hair out as I tried to say the lines of the Tablet of Ahmad. I could almost feel the misty darkness around me, as if I were cloaked in some nether world. Agonizing over what I should do, where I should go, I stumbled into a rose bush with one rose in bloom. It was almost comic. Where could I be, I wondered, where there is a rose bush? I picked the one rose on the bush and smelled its delicate sweetness, and immediately I thought of 'Abdu'l-Bahá. My spirit was once again in Haifa on pilgrimage, the fragrance of rose petals from the Shrines wafting in the air. Then I noticed the gentle swishing of the ocean waves near my feet. I had been led blindly, in darkness, to the ocean of God's mercy. In a sense—to God. All things merged into nothingness before Him; I clung to the Cord. I could hardly see, but I wanted to walk along the shoreline, to gaze out into the ocean, into infinity. I wanted assurance from the breakers, lapping one upon another in perpetual motion, that the steady movement of the sea onto land would reinforce the movement of my life and my hopes for surer direction. I wanted as much of this as possible, before ending years and years of marriage and returning home to St. Louis.

I had been afraid. Afraid to take risks, to lose face, to start over, to suffer material loss. But now I sensed my depression had become an empowering path to a more inner-directed person. Torn between the words of the Guardian condemning divorce and my own inner feelings, I had finally come to recognize that the essence of my being was put there by God. Getting in touch with it and knowing more about myself was a new dimension in growth. I had to give in to it, to ignore the surface. There was more to the story than an image, a mask, a persona. Like the story of the man who went in search around the world for Truth, only to return home and find it within a walnut shell.

Everyone must make her own inner journey. I had found myself. That was the moment I made a conscious choice. No more conflict, no more vacillation or anxiety. I took the responsibility of decision for direction and wellness. The depression was not yet over, but I was grounded in a newer, better relationship in knowing God: following the river to the ocean, I had become one with the river. I had been driven to go someplace where I could get in touch with my spiritual Self. It was only one aspect of recovery, but perhaps a key one.

The Value of Depression. If looking for the source of depression is like looking into a crystal ball, finding the solution is as difficult. Solutions are varied and multidimensional; a person's own input is needed. Regardless of origin or treatment, the key understanding may be that depression is a valid step in spiritual development. The more we know about ourselves, the better we can make choices and maintain mental wellness. We have the Writings and the laws of the Revelators as guidelines. These laws represent divine Love, the motivating power of all creation, a love that lifts us up to a position of dignity and shows us that our true nature is spiritual; our essence, the essence of God. It may be necessary, however, to get help in our efforts to know ourselves in order that each individual can take charge of the personal struggle.

The test of depression is the challenge. I have often wondered if the mental turmoil of depression might be one of the severe mental tests which the Guardian said would inevitably sweep over the believers of the West: "tests that would purge, purify and prepare them for their noble mission in life."[35]

One day, while pondering this question, I found a prayer from the Báb which says: "I know of a certainty, by virtue of my love for Thee, that Thou wilt never cause tribulations to befall any soul unless Thou desirest to exalt his station in Thy celestial Paradise and to buttress his heart . . . that it may not become inclined toward the vanities of this world."[36] I took this quote to mean that we are not victims of depression, but rather that we are challenged to transcend it. With God, there are no victims. It is what one does with depression that matters. Many great writers and artists have worked through depression to give us a glimpse of some larger truth about man's noble and tragic experience.

The affliction is universal. It goes back to Biblical times, to King Saul and Job. Writers such as Dostoevski and Blake, artists like Van Gogh and Gauguin offer insights into the beauty and depravity of man. Victor Frankl writes that there were two brothers, identical twins, who suffered with endogenous depression. One turned to crime; the other to helping society as a criminologist.[37] How one reacts to situations, then, is the value into which he has molded his suffering; it is his personal creation, his bestowal of meaning to his suffering, says Frankl.

Frankl, like many of the Existentialist thinkers, experienced the death and darkness of concentration camps. They knew depression. Yet, out of those terrible conditions came their message to look within to what they called the inner light, a spark of God in every man, but this true reality cannot be found if one is alienated from his spiritual nature. In The Hidden Words, Bahá'u'lláh writes: *"I have breathed within thee a breath of My own Spirit,"* and, *"Turn thy sight unto thyself, that thou mayest find Me standing within thee, mighty, powerful and self-subsisting."*[38]

Martin Buber, the Jewish existentialist, refers to this inner light as the *indwelling* of God, a term influenced by Jewish mysticism. "The human world," he wrote, "is meant to become a single body through the actions of men themselves."[39] As Bahá'ís, if we are to become one soul in many bodies, then surely, as spiritual beings, as followers of the Light, universally sensitive to the pain and suffering of others as we experience the spiritualizing process of tearing down the old world order so as to build the new— then surely we can help one another transcend the darkness. In a basic sense, our very existence depends on an accurate understanding of our spiritual nature which Bahá'u'lláh brings. For without this knowledge of God and man's relation to Him we cannot banish the rigid, negative thoughts and actions of former generations. And we certainly cannot solve our difficulties without the healing Message that the divine Manifestation brings.

As we redirect our thinking and investigate productive ways to develop the powers which Bahá'u'lláh tells us we have to develop, we can consider a point that 'Abdu'l-Bahá stressed: *"Do not look at your weakness, nay, rely upon the confirmation of the Holy Spirit. Verily it maketh the weak strong, the lowly mighty . . . and the small great."*[40]

Notes and References

1. Nathan S. Kline, M.D., *From Sad to Glad* (New York: Ballantine Books, 1974) p. 74 [The synapse is 1/100,000,000th of an inch in measurement; amines flash across at 1/1,000th of a second].

2. The depression syndrome, he said, is characterized both by physical disorders, such as headaches, gastritis/colitis, and by a host of mood disturbances and anxieties. The warning flags of depression include the following: feelings of worthlessness and helplessness; agoraphobia, the fear of socializing; continuous agitation or hostility; overconcern or obsession with a problem; anger when one is asked to make decisions; fatigue and prolonged lack of motivation; change of eating or sleeping patterns; crying for no apparent reason; loss of feelings of love and affection; talk of suicide.

When a person's mood swings back and forth from normal to depressed, the affliction is called unipolar; however, when mood swings are from normal to *hopped up*, or from depressed to high, the illness is bipolar: that is called manic-depressive. Even the person with unipolar type can have an isolated phase of mania. In the overactive, manic phase, nerve activity within the brain is speeded up. At these times a person may go on wild spending sprees, or exhibit in a number of other ways the ebullient action of what author Dr. Leonard Cammer calls a *human dynamo*, never sleeping, overloaded with ideas, feeling great. Some women and men leave their families; others become hyperactive in political and religious activities.

Excellent lists and explanation of depression symptoms can be found in the following: Dr. Nathan S. Kline, *From Sad to Glad* (Ballantine Books, 1979); Dr. David D. Burns, *Feeling Good* (Signet, 1981); Dr. John White, *The Masks of Melancholy* (Signet, 1982); Dr. Helen A. De Rosis and Victoria Y. Pellegrino, *The Book of Hope* (Bantam Books, 1981).

3. Depression is a very complex illness, as it may involve

many aspects of stress, one compounded upon another. Why one person is able to handle stress better than another is not fully understood. But, as one psychiatrist explains, individuals who have a biochemical problem to start with would be highly susceptible to stress factors that might affect the biological balance of their brain chemistry. Scientists continue to work to make advances in determining which amino acids help the body produce norepinephrine and the other amines needed for neurotransmitters and to determine how allergic reactions can alter the brain chemistry. Some experts feel that, with more information, good nutrition can help ward off depression and other illnesses; others, however, fail to see any connection.

In a talk to the American Schizophrenic Association, Dr. Tipu Sultan, Environmental Allergist, Pediatrician, and Medical Director of the St. Louis Center for Preventive Medicine, explained that the three major hidden factors in clinical depression today, for both men and women, are 1) Hypothyroidism (or low thyroid); 2) Allergies to foods and chemicals; and 3) Candidiasis (or yeast infection).

Unfortunately, detection and isolation of these three hidden factors can be extremely difficult, for there is a wide range of normal thyroid levels among individuals, and their symptoms (which include migraine-like headaches, hormone changes, fatigue, depression, anxiety, constipation or diarrhea, colitis, cystitis, sinusitis, and others) are common to many illnesses. Because yeast cells live naturally in the body, Candida overgrowth and accompanying toxins can easily be intensified by rounds of antibiotics, birth control pills, steroids, chemotherapy, prolonged carbohydrate/sugar diet, and repeated pregnancies. An April 1986 *Redbook* article included an anti-yeast diet and a list of organizations which provide further information.

In studies on biochemical changes related to allergies, clinical allergists report that, just as an allergy can bring about tissue changes in the mucous membranes, they can also alter brain chemistry. Dr. Robert Forman, author of a book on bioecologic disorders, cites examples of depression, disorientation, and psychotic symptoms as examples of psychiatric and other allergy-based medical problems. When depression has actually been caused by the allergic reaction, the depression will subside when the person is no longer in contact with the allergen. On the other hand, when depression is only complicated by allergy factors, as in the case of a Harvard graduate student who was found to be allergic to milk and other foods, it is still necessary to continue antidepressants, or other therapy, even after eliminating the allergy-causing foods from the diet.

Two other depression-related diseases where diet is crucial include hypoglycemia, or low blood sugar, and Pre-Menstrual Syndrome (PMS). In hypoglycemia, diet is used to regulate the level of blood sugar, as in the diabetic diet. In PMS, doctors studying factors related to PMS symptoms have developed an entire procedure which often alleviates depression and other emotional difficulties through diet, Vitamin B6 supplements and, when necessary, the administration of minute doses of natural progesterone. The synthetic progesterone used in birth control pills can bring about mood swings by counteracting the effect of natural progesterone, an important part of the body's own defense against depression. In fact, one woman reported that her depression symptoms had been alleviated to a great degree as if by accident when she discontinued her prescription for birth-control pills. Even though she had been hospitalized for depression, her doctors had given her a prescription which, they assured her, was not supposed to contribute to depression; but even that was apparently too much.

There seems to be no argument that diet is important in helping the body build resistance to illness. Eating properly decreases the internal state of susceptibility that predisposes a person to become sick. Some psychiatrists claim that junk food, with excessive salts and sugars, is one of the elements that can contribute to stress on the body; and stress is just one more compounding effect that may alter a person's mood. One doctor in Florida, involved in ascertaining which nutrients help in the body's production of amines for neurotransmitters, has had great success with a combination of L-tyrozine, vitamin C, niacinimide, and vitamin B6, taken to supplement a well-balanced diet. Several patients on antidepressants who have consulted him regarding the combination have reported that they have been able to lower the amount of medication they had been taking, with their doctor's approval, and, in turn, have had less side effects from their medication.

Besides allergy testing and nutritional concerns, there are two important components of supplementing therapy which can prove helpful. They are exercise and meditation. The discipline of regular exercise helps psychologically, but there is also a physical benefit that is mood elevating. Many researchers claim that exercise increases the level of endorphins within the bloodstream, a substance which is biochemically similar to morphine, and which has been referred to as the body's natural opiate in helping the body adapt to stress. But meditation and relaxation techniques may also be beneficial because they raise endorphin levels as well as cut out bombardment of worrisome thoughts and noises, as pointed out in *Relaxation Response*.

4. Leonard Cammer, M.D., *Up from Depression* (New York: Pocket Books, 1971) p. 47.

5. Deborah Belle, ed., *Lives in Stress: Women and Depression* (Beverly Hills, CA: Sage, 1980), pp. 198–9.

6. Kline, p. 12.

7. Cammer, p. 17.

8. Ebrahim Amanat, M.D., "Adolescent Depression, Covert Anger, and Suicide," *Res Medica*, Vol. 3, No. 2 (Fall 1986), p. 5.

9. Farzaneh Guillebeaux, M.A., personal phone interview, Montgomery, Alabama, January 5, 1987.

10. Ebrahim Amanat, M.D. and Ann Wiebmer, R.N. M.S.N., "Women's Integrity Trauma Syndrome," *Family Therapy*, Vol. 12, No. 3, (1985) pp. 253–4.

11. Ibid.

12. Nancy Chodorow, "Being and Doing: A Cross-Cultural Examination of the Socialization of Males and Females," in Vivian Gornick and Barbara K. Moran, eds. *Woman in Sexist Society* (New York: Basic Books, 1971) p. 193.

13. Helen A. De Rosis, M.D. and Victoria Y. Pellegrino, *The Book of Hope* (New York: Bantam Books, 1981) p. 99.

14. Marzieh Gail, M.A., *Dawn Over Mount Hira* (Oxford: George Ronald, U.S. Printing, 1976) p. 141.

15. Natalie Shainess, M.D., *Sweet Suffering: Woman as Victim* (New York: Bobbs-Merrill, 1984) p. 8.

16. De Rosis and Pellegrino, p. 88.

17. Ann Schoonmaker, *Me, Myself, and I* (New York and Toronto: Harper and Row, 1977) p. 22–3.

18. Shainess, p. 23.

19. Ibid., p. 3.

20. Ibid.

21. Pauline Bart, "Depression in Middle-aged Women," in Vivian Gornick and Barbara Moral, eds., *Woman in Sexist Society* (New York: Basic Books, 1971) p. 104.

22. Ibid., p. 101.

23. Farzaneh Guillebeaux, "The Background and Decision Making of Males Participating in Marriage and Family Therapy," Auburn University Thesis, Auburn, 1984, p. 9.

24. Guillebeaux, p. 7.

25. Ibid., pp. 8–9.

26. Guillebeaux, pp. 14–15.

27. Gloria Steinem, "What It Would Be Like If Women Win," In Diana Reische, ed., *Women in Society* (New York: Wilson Co., 1972) [reprinted from *Time* 96: 22–23].

28. Guillebeaux, pp. 19–20.

29. Ibid., pp. 67–68.

30. Farzaneh Guillebeaux, M.A., personal phone interview, Montgomery, Alabama, January 8, 1987.

31. Ibid.

32. Arnold Nerenberg, Ph.D., *Love and Estrangement in the Bahá'í Community*, (Los Angeles: Kalimát Press, 1985), pp. 21–23.

33. Bahá'u'lláh, *Gleanings*, pp. 164–5.

34. Ibid.

35. Helen Hornby, ed., *Lights of Guidance, A Bahá'í Reference*, (New Delhi, India: Bahá'í Publishing Trust, 1983) p. 94.

36. *Bahá'í Prayers*, (Wilmette, Ill.: Bahá'í Publishing Trust, 1985) p. 194.

37. Frankl, p. 49.

38. *The Hidden Words of Bahá'u'lláh*, translated by Shoghi Effendi (Wilmette, Ill.: Bahá'í Publishing Committee, 1954) p. 8, Verse 19 and p. 7, Verse 13.

39. William Robert Miller, "Personalistic Philosophy of Hope," *Saturday Review* (Feb. 10, 1968) p. 34.

40. *The Divine Art of Living*, Mabel Hyde Paine, ed. (Wilmette, Ill.: Bahá'í Publishing Trust, 1944) p. 46.

In *The Hidden Words*, pp. 6–7, are found references to God's essence in man ("Thou art My Lamp . . . , within thee have I placed the essence of My light . . . , Thou art My dominion . . . , Thou art My light . . . , Thou art My glory . . . ")

Year(s) of Patience

by Esther Bradley

I HAD A HOLE in my soul. I either scratched it on a rock on the bottom of the Ocean of Preexistence, caught it on a gossamer wing on the trip out, or my twin sister, Liz, sat on me during the prebirth process. This hole has given me some trouble.

Eight years after becoming a Bahá'í, and six months into my Year of Patience, the hole in my soul burst. Confused messages about my place in the world, first as a girl growing up in the forties and fifties, then as a woman in the sixties, puzzled me. I would come to the realization that the "Year of Patience" is not a simple year to clock into on January 1, and clock out at midnight the following December 31. My Year of Patience lasted ten years. I had to deal with issues, collective and personal, that lay within me and were formed long before I became a Bahá'í. My most problematic angst was the hole in my soul: the void I had always felt.

Childhood clopped by in turbulent fashion. Liz and I arrived in West Roxbury, Massachusetts in 1938. We were the last of four children ("Good grief, girls!") born within three years. Liz was blond, blue-eyed, roly-poly. I was clinging to four pounds and looked like a squirrel shoved out of its mother's nest too soon.

In our house on Wren Street, adults, kids, dogs, and cats lived squished together in tense abandon. We were an Irish Catholic household tinged with alcoholism. We would survive air raid sirens, blackouts, and World War II. Ours was a nation coming of age. Margarine was discovered; lard, the old standby, was put aside forever. Chlorophyll promised to sweeten dogs' breath. Television found a waiting audience. Women were to discover themselves. Despite magazine articles urging them back to home and hearth, they felt differently. Women in the fifties realized that they weren't Betty Grable, didn't want to be Betty Crocker, and didn't have to talk like Betty Boop. Maybe, just maybe, if they didn't say "What do you think, dear?" to their husbands, they would still get through the day.

Childhood gave me an eclectic view. We could roller skate through the house during the day, but we had to be in bed early for the grownups' nightly cocktail ritual. I felt a little uneasy. But I kept on the move, prowling about the neighborhood of Wren and Oriole Streets with a nose that cast long shadows on the cracks of the sidewalk and kneecaps that would take years to grow into.

Women from my mother's era, except for maybe Eleanor Roosevelt, weren't too defined. My mother's wit and conversation were stuffed with wry little sayings and a bemused, saddened view of life. I thought my mother was nifty. So did her fellow teachers at the Randall G. Morris Elementary School where we, her Bradley twins, went to school. My father didn't agree. "The family falls apart when the woman works" was his oft-repeated edict.

Catholicism formed my collective view: Women named Mary suffer the most. Mothers bear the most pain and are the most selfless. A woman's most painful, yet most joyous moment is in giving birth. ·

My mother's name was Mary. After our days at the beach, when we were full of grit and grime, she would wait to shower last. Even our dog Chocla and Benny, our cat, would eat before she would. My older sister, who later bottomed out on alcohol for ten years, was also named Mary.

Homemaking class at school gave us Miss Montana. She looked nothing like a beauty queen and never won an award for anything except for tidiness. Miss Montana looked like a flamenco dancer. She had a clear, uncompromising view of world order: "A place for everything and everything in its place." In a sprawling old yellow house across from the First National Bank, on Centre Street, Harry Raymond's Ballroom Dancing School prepared us socially. Harry, who gadded about like an opaque crow, admonished: "Women do not sit with their legs apart."

As a girl-child of the fifties, sitting on the bench at Harry's waiting to be asked for a dance, I had time to mope and muse about my future. Vistas of dreamed-for marriage, service rendered through the home, loomed. No other way of life was imagined.

But at twenty-four, my nose sort of settled into my face, and my kneecaps no longer looked like the backsides of twin turtles. Ballroom dancing, along with Harry and Miss Montana, were shadows. I left Massachusetts and the memories of a mother dying early and a father disillusioned by life. Any serious thoughts I had were hidden under quick quips and a lot of drinking. Fear of life surfaced now and again. Whenever I dated men in Brooks Brothers suits, I tossed down Compose and alcohol. Therapy beckoned at age twenty-five, and I married at age twenty-six. At a bar on Sunset Boulevard, as the twilight waned, my husband-to-be and I took care of life's details. He promised that we would "raise the children Catholic." The following year I found the Bahá'í Faith.

Life changed.

"How am I going to give up drinking?" I fretted. A friend said, "Honey, don't worry about it. It will give you up." Sure enough, my penchant for scotch and soda left me in a hurry, like an eight-legged insect scurrying away from the Raid can. I fought my spiritual battles and trotted down the beginning paths of the Faith I had newly embraced. Like someone who had lived in a land of black and white hopscotch, it seemed I had stumbled across a multihued pathway.

I was not a homemaking star. Along with mediocre dinners, I cooked a couple of instruction books to aluminum pans. I cringed with shame when chastised for "being out of toilet paper." But still, I was married. The forties and fifties voice within me demanded that a woman be married.

As I deepened in the Bahá'í writings, became part of the Bahá'í community, sought the sanctuary of prayers, I grew strong. Where I had been dependent and fearful, relying on others for "What do you think," I found my own standards. A sense of self-certitude grew. My husband was not a Bahá'í. This helped foster my sense of independence. Disunity between us about the Faith was something I guarded against. But, had he been a Bahá'í, I think I would have leaned on him unnecessarily.

I sought my father's view. I mailed him a copy of *Bahá'u'lláh and the New Era*, passionately underlined in red pencil by me. His only cryptic reply: "I know all about the Bábís," ended any further dialogue between us about the Faith. Thus it became necessary for me not to lean. While I did not find emotional independence easy, my steadfastness grew. I came to a strong appreciation of our planet's pole vault into maturity, and I felt both pride and gratitude for being a small part of the process.

While I finally learned to tidy up around the house enough to satisfy even Miss Montana, life via marriage was imposing terse conditions. When giant words like "LOST YOUR JOB," "DRINK TOO MUCH," and "LONELINESS WITHIN MARRIAGE" invaded my life, the walls and I stuck together. There followed many chapters of "A Bahá'í Goes to Marriage Counseling."

I didn't want to divorce. To the same friend who had

counseled me about drinking, I asked in a bewildered moment: "What happened?"

"Honey," she said, "you leaned on him, and he fell over."

Sore knees and thousands of prayers later led me to the realization that a silent *no* seemed to be forming in the universe. That *no* was about my marriage. If I did not leave my husband, he would never get up. But other thoughts nagged me. I was afraid to be alone. Unwillingness to face a future by myself nudged my bone marrow.

The Bahá'í Faith had been the light switch to my universe. Despite personal tests, I found my Bahá'í life richly solid and satisfying. I traveled about with friends who were drunk on the wine of steadfastness and service. My women friends were an odd collection of gutsy ladies who had the courage to be different—to say, "Yes. I'm a Bahá'í." (Then, not many people knew the name. The standard response would be, "You're a whoooo?") We marched along with a kind of inner "nobodysgoingtorainonmyparade" attitude. I gained enormous strength from them.

So my Year of Patience was a surprise to me. I was mute, mindless, screaming, vocal, bizarre. I was to be everything that I had not been.

The hole in my soul split open.

"What's a Year of Patience?" friends unfamiliar with the Faith would ask.

"Well," I'd ask, scratching my head, "I think it's a time to heal. You separate, you don't date anyone. If the marriage is to work, it will. Hopefully, you both—given time and distance—see things with new eyes. You get your dignity back . . . I don't think you would have an intense affair with anyone. But, maybe a cup of coffee is okay."

I couldn't find much written on the Year of Patience. I studied *Fortress of Well-Being*. Divorce is strongly discouraged. I knew that it was considered as a "last resort only in the case of extreme aversion and irreparable disunity, when all other means of reconciliation" had failed.

That was my marriage. I went to the local Spiritual Assembly. I knew that the conditions of the Year of Patience meant I had to be "patient and wait for one complete year. If during this year harmony is not reestablished, . . . then divorce may be realized."

The Assembly was fair and considerate to both my husband and myself. He, while packing his jelly glasses from the 1920s warned me darkly: "I'm going to tell them *everything* about you." He went to the Assembly. They reported back to me; Norma was the spokesperson.

"Well," she said, nervously clearing her throat, "it seems there are *things* in your refrigerator somewhere between the state of gas and mold. They move."

"Is that it?" I died inwardly. (Refrigerators had always been difficult. Sometimes the stuff simply got away from me. The innards smelled like day's end at a cheese factory in the Alps. "Is Heidi in there?" friends would wonder.)

"Seems to be," Norma replied.

The civil side of divorce had to be dealt with. I had not brought any cows to the marriage. Had I, they would have been barbecued long before. But despite the lack of possessions, friends urged me, "Get an attorney." "What for?" I said, "I can do it myself." Somehow, though, the pink financial forms felled me. I went to an attorney. He reviewed my circumstances. "Pay me five dollars a month," he offered. Three years later, I sent in my last $5 mailing.

Emotionally I had expectations. Naively, I began my singlehood with: (1) I won't be lonely; (2) My Faith and Bahá'í activities will sustain me; (3) God will reward me with a good man; and (4) God will reward me *soon*. Sure, tests and difficulties would still be there, but life would have clarity. Like those mythical creatures in the last chapters of self-help books, I would march through the year wrapped in a cloak of spiritual security, armed with fortitude. I would be secure, because I was a Bahá'í. I would be happy to be active. I would be cushioned from my aloneness.

So I thought.

The first three or four months it worked that way. I sallied forth and discovered a small apartment in a beach town hiding amidst trees, tucked in a back alley. The Bahá'í community was relatively large. They were active and loving. The town was quaint, small, and funky. The apartment was the same. A huge window looked onto a sprawling oak tree.

I had been lonely, terribly lonely, while married. The Faith had eased much inner pain. I had no reason to believe this would not continue. In fact, the move would make my life easier. After work, on weekends, I took ferryboat rides, I burrowed in and out of bookstores, played in the sand. I juggled finances and went about my business.

Suddenly time crept up on me. For no explainable reason, my routine stopped functioning. I tentatively queried people. It seemed that no one had the answers—least of all people who had never been divorced. I was bewildered. Pain hit me whenever I opened the door to my tiny house. Unexpected loneliness clogged in my throat. I felt conflict. As a Bahá'í, I should be shored up, secure, I reasoned. Something is wrong. I had other friends who were going through the same thing. They had no answers either. I panicked. I'm defective, I thought. If the Faith isn't sustaining me, I'm not spiritual.

One day in this frame of mind I wandered down to the center of town. I was at loose ends. I looked in bookstore windows. I walked. All around me the street bustled with activity. I thought of a conversation the previous evening with a Bahá'í: "Gee, it must be terrific to have all that time to read."

Silently, I had wondered: But what about the abyss, the hole? Where is that from?

Someone else had said, "Yeah, it would be great to walk the beach all by yourself."

I nodded, and I understood. But they didn't understand

that you could walk the beach alone today, tomorrow, and for the next ten thousand Tuesdays. It was scary. There were no signposts.

In this frame of mind, I wandered over to a bench outside of a doughnut shop and mused over a cup of coffee. A shadow fell over me. I looked up to the voice which said, "Well, you're a surprise." My family doctor who had seen me through viruses, flus, and shaky times smiled down at me. "I'm glad to see you. I was afraid you'd never talk to me again."

I was glad I was sitting down, for I remembered with all too much clarity what he was talking about. A year before, while I was in the last awful stages of my marriage, I had run into this man, this family doctor, this pillar of advice. He had told me, over coffee in a half-deserted hospital cafeteria, that I had "the soul of an artist," that he was "attracted" to me, that I "made his day" whenever I came into his office. I felt like Margaret O'Brien, the child movie star with a sweet, high-pitched voice and braids. She believed everything. I was no different. That night, across the room from the line of string beans, jellos, and puddings, it took me a full thirty minutes to realize that this man was propositioning *me*. My heart sat in my throat. Somehow I managed to say, swinging my invisible Margaret O'Brien braids aside, "Look, um, I'm married, and I'm a Bahá'í. It's mostly that. You wouldn't understand. I can't get involved."

We parted, walked out of the cafeteria toward the parking lot together. His arm rested across my shoulders. Even then, I remember the human touch was wonderful. I was beginning to think about then that the only meaningful touch for me would be the dentist's hairy fist moving his drill across my face, and saying, "You can rinse now." That night, as I watched him walking into a night and a life that I imagined filled with sophisticated happenings, I felt empty.

And so a year later, six months into my Year of Patience,

I clutched my coffee cup and looked at this man.

I clutched my coffee cup and looked at this man. He sat next to me on the bench by the doughnut shop. We talked. I filled my eyes with him: tall, silver-haired, eyes peeping over Benjamin Franklin glasses, a firm mouth telling me, "Yes, you will feel loneliness. But those who like you will really care." We talked again of his marriage, his loneliness. He was still married. "I'll never remarry," he said. "But you must. You are far too young not to." He asked me to dinner, saying, "This relationship can be anything you want it to be. I know you, your standards. I like the spiritual side of you. But still, could we have dinner tonight?"

I looked at him. He was a combination of Ashley Wilkes, Rhett Butler, and Heathcliff. I didn't know whether to say, "I can't live without you; Atlanta is burning," or "Take me to the window, Heathcliff." That sunny afternoon the world seemed full of smiling couples. I went to dinner.

Dinner became more than dinner. I moved into this relationship like a willing victim numbed into a spider's nest. Later, in my room, I kept imagining 'Abdu'l-Bahá shaking his head sadly. I put my prayerbook away. I felt too numb to pray. Later, friends said *don't*, so I started to pray again.

I struggled with my feelings of unworthiness and stayed active in the community. I would struggle within this relationship to finally become horrified at my own dependency, my need for validation. I was already thin, I lost weight. I cried in unexplained places. Emotional control left my vocabulary. Guilt and need clashed within me. This man and I were stellar opposites. He was prominent in the city: my addled social self was dazzled. He was emotionally contained: I was Isadora Duncan on a binge. He needed no one: I needed everyone. So it went—I was a marionnette.

My need to be held was insatiable. My guilt was insane. The relationship he had said could be "anything I wanted," dictated and drove me. It was nothing I needed and everything I clung to.

As the months went by, pain eclipsed me. I thought of his

wife. Despite his "She doesn't know," I hated the deceit. I hated hurting another woman. I hated the whole thing. I ended the affair.

For the next ten days I couldn't sleep. I went around in a daze. I called a friend and started to cry. "I can't do it, Sue. I can't give him up."

"Some people can't give up alcohol either," she answered.

Something clicked. I had never really forgiven my mother for being an alcoholic. She had died when I was a teenager. I was nasty and critical. I had been even more critical of my father. I hated his allowing my mother's obsession to kill us all. Yet obsession in another form now visited me.

The next day, a sunny Saturday morning, I picked up a pillow, stuffed it against my mouth, and screamed. My room was empty; my house was empty; my entire world was vacant. My soul felt like ice. I went to the phone, dialed a number that would end my emptiness. "I think I have a bleeding ulcer" got me past the doctor's answering service, beyond his hello, his family's laughter in the background.

My barely whispered "I have to see you," collided with his cheery, detached That-would-be-quite-nice-Why-not-get-together-for-tea voice. The absence had been torture for me, time spent in a concentration camp. Not so for my significant other. He had been mildly irritated. I finally began to glimpse a view of myself as a toy—a nice one, but a toy. Each new insight was uncomfortable, painful, shamefilled.

His marriage ended, not by my doing. Paradoxically, he had less time for me, more time for others: an interior designer, another doctor. I felt the bite of class prejudice. My inner Irish survivor that had been playing doormat for months arose. He pleasantly responded to my wrath: "I'm not capable of having deep feelings for you anymore." I was aghast, I was relieved. What then? Emma Bovary took rat poison. I had more options.

It took two years to heal. I would move into a small community and surround myself with friends. A relative lent me the money to buy a small house. I got a scruffy dog from a pet orphanage. We went on long walks. I discovered bike riding and running. The community of Bahá'ís was small, active, and nurturing. We laughed a lot. Owning a house gave me a sense of "Heyicandoit!" My needs, so maniacally channeled into I-can't-live-without-him, took tentative new pathways.

I knew I had passed my test when a year later, on my way to a Bahá'í gathering, I was in an automobile accident. I didn't see the red sports car coming towards me. He was going 60 miles an hour. We hit. Time froze. We spun round and round. I took the rear view mirror off with my head. Blood gushed from my scalp, my cheek was cut, my neck was injured. The paramedics laid me on a stretcher on the ground. "We're going to take you to the hospital," one of them said as he placed a neck support under my head. "Do you have a doctor?"

"No," I said.

I hope I got a merit badge for that. I had rough physical moments ahead, with long days and weeks of physical therapy. I lost my job, I had totaled my car. But I was grateful. That accident and my *no* had closed my need always to cling. I survived.

I enrolled in college. I stopped dating; my ego had been ground into the mud. I claimed myself. It was a long process, but four years of college changed me. I saw a therapist. I began just to have friends, male and female. I learned to trust, I learned to feed myself, to feed my soul.

There were many ways to start looking at the hole in my soul. I could laugh when my therapist insisted, "You're a bird looking for a cage." But it didn't matter. I was no longer devastated because I was alone.

As the university years went by, I found a particular inner food I valued: the literature of contemporary women. I had always read a lot, but the writers I discovered validated the women of this time. We are facing and initiating change in this new age. Loneliness is one of the prices we pay for being a part of the creative minority in society. Having the Bahá'í viewpoint, seeing the broad spectrum, helped. It didn't always make it easy. Sometimes vulnerability and loneliness bit like a python.

The hole in my soul mended. It mended on threads of stuff like Mozart, coffee and doughnuts with good friends, the struggles of learning French. It was the thrill of having my stories read in class; the silent pleasure of running a track at ten o'clock in the morning; the simplicity of walking to classes in the fresh air carrying books on Hopkins and Blake. And the gutsiness of women going back to university struck me. We were eccentric, fun-loving, driven. None of us had money. We were all tired, some of us had been really sick. But we were a fierce bunch who had life plans that would keep us busy until the year 2052.

I would look back and laugh at my thoughts: God will reward me with a good man *soon*. Even God, I chuckled, would have difficulties finding a good man in California. Besides, I wasn't afraid of being alone anymore. I was no longer the waxen tablet desperate for a relationship stamp. I still missed the holding. But, I didn't miss demeaning myself. Gradually, instead of being a human pretzel, twisted into a pleasing shape, I started listening to myself and my needs. I let go of expectations.

Sure there were slips—like the night a man cooked me dinner, nagging and criticizing me the whole evening. Inwardly, I was livid. Outwardly, I sounded like Marabel Morgan, the Total Woman advocate. "This is very nice meat loaf," I said, as he looked at me with sour distaste. And I said it at least five times.

I had good days and bad days. Slowly, oh so slowly, the hole in my soul closed. And one day, while I was whizzing through life looking the other way, a man with a tattered tag labeled "Soon" and "Not from California" appeared in my path. I fell in love with him. When we met, he said, "I like your tie." We talked at Feast, we hung out at District Convention. We married three months later.

There is still my personality to deal with. Some people have freckles. Some have warts. While reading a draft of this essay, my husband remarked, "I've been meaning to talk to you about the refrigerator."

I wonder as I write: Am I still vulnerable? The answer, of course, is yes. But would I, if left alone again, revert? My life is wondrously full now. It was also wondrously full these last ten years. Becoming single, being tired, lonely, probably not hungry, but all that other stuff—moments of wanting to bay at the moon, moments of wanting to go out into the garden and eat worms—all those times formed me. I would have it no other way.

And so it is, the end of an episode. I still wobble a bit. I sort of tilt towards Massachusetts when I pray. Maybe that's the patchwork on my soul.

Gender Relations:
A Cross-Cultural Dilemma

by Peggy Caton

"WHY CAN'T A WOMAN be more like a man?" laments many a Professor Higgins past and present. "Vive la différence!" reply a myriad Chevaliers, escorting their Gigis along the promenade.

And how many unsung women have wished secretly that men were more like women?

Many men and women do not really understand or like each other, although they depend on the other sex for the qualities and services they provide. Although each sex is conditioned to perform different roles and behaviors, often they both wish the other were more like themselves.

Relations between the sexes mirror the difficulties and problems associated with relations between different cultures, particularly cultures with a history of uneven power relations, such as Britain and colonial India or black and white America. Masculinity and femininity really spring from two different cultural or subcultural systems, each with its own values, goals, and styles of communication. Male-female relations reflect these cross-cultural differences, and also reveal differences in power, roles, and expectations.

This essay discusses these differences and their implications for understanding inequality between the sexes. It proposes a communications model based on the idea of men and women sharing power, values, and personality traits formerly assigned only to one or the other of them. This model would allow for individual and for gender differences, but not those created by inequality of power or assigned and limited roles and personalities.

Cross-cultural studies have found no absolute personality differences between men and women that exist in all societies. In some cultures both men and women are more like either the male or the female type in our society. For example, both may be gentle, or both aggressive. In some cases there is trait reversal, depending on what a society considers desirable and appropriate.[1] In one society it is the women who carry heavy loads and the men who are considered gossips.[2]

Margaret Mead's study of three different societies in New Guinea found one group in which both men and women are cooperative and gentle; another where both are aggressive and violent; and a third in which men and women had different and complementary temperaments, but reversed from what is traditional in Western European societies.[3] The women controlled production and were regarded as stable, dominant, unemotional, and highly sexed. The men were emotionally volatile, highly adorned, dependent, and sexually passive. Although the men retained official control of the society and would resort to physical violence when they felt it necessary, their main role was to stage elaborate music and dance ceremonies for the benefit of the women.

Many studies conducted in the United States indicate, however, that males may be innately more aggressive than females.[4] In this country, this trait is cultivated by social patterns that permit males to display direct aggression.[5] In general, women's position as mother has oriented her towards home and family, and her status in society has been assigned on the basis of this biological role.[6] This role has often kept her from greater participation and achievement in the public sphere of society. Women relate to each other in an egalitarian manner, based on the relative similarity of their roles within their respective cultures.[7]

Men, however, are associated with the creation and transmission of cultural systems, and a nation is judged most often by the behavior of its dominant men.[8] Men develop hierarchies of dominance based on achievement within the social order they have created.[9]

We derive many of our current Western attitudes toward the roles and personality traits of men and women from the changes brought about by industrialization. Toffler, author of *Future Shock* and *The Third Wave*, proposes that in agricultural societies both men and women work at home. As a result of the Industrial Revolution, men were forced to leave home to work in factories. They soon discovered that the skills and personality traits required for individualized home production were not appropriate in factory work. A worker in an agricultural society performed a variety of tasks according to a relatively flexible schedule. Products were hand-crafted and designed, often by a single worker. In contrast, an industrial worker had to be objective and precise, producing standardized goods as one specialized unit in a highly coordinated and efficient system. By remaining at home, women retained the more personalized and flexible agrarian life-style.[10]

Toffler believes that male-female differences in the industrialized West stem from the difference between agrarian and industrial economic requirements. In the United States, the female value system is similar to that of certain non-American cultures in, for example, its emphasis on group identity, harmony with nature, and interdependence.[11]

The industrial society found this new split of public and

private spheres as necessary to support a well-functioning economy.[12] Women at home raised children and provided a nurturing environment for the men, who traveled to their jobs and worked long, concentrated hours. This pattern became the basis for much of our current thinking of men as task-oriented, or instrumental; and of women as emotional, or expressive.[13] We have forgotten that this is a relatively new phenomenon within our own culture. Nor have we turned to other societies to recognize the wide variety of temperaments expressed in human cultures.

Alternative Value System. Within American society, there are two basic value systems: the dominant system, represented by males of higher status and rank, and a variant or alternative system represented by females and other low-status groups.[14] This alternative value system exists within, and supports, the framework of male values which is used to define American society.[15]

The male focuses on himself as a creative and active individual, while the female focuses on her responsiveness to and harmony with others:

Male Type	*Female Type*
instrumental	affective
active	passive
doing	being
verbal	nonverbal
aggressive	supportive
domineering	submissive
individual achievement	group identity
self-concerned	responsive
demanding	accommodating
independent	interdependent
external evaluation	self-actualization
future time	present time
conquest of nature	harmony with nature

According to a study by Carol Gilligan, society defines the male identity as its standard.[16] For example, U.S. psychologists consider male ethics (although not identified as such) as more mature than female morality.[17]

Let us take a hypothetical situation in the Bahá'í community: Someone has been observed drinking alcohol. According to Gilligan's theory, a male would see to it that the law-breaker was duly reported to the local Assembly, treated according to established guidelines, and that he receive the same treatment as anyone else in this situation. The male would typically make sure that in reporting the person to the Assembly none of his own rights (to confidentiality, perhaps) were violated and that he was not violating anyone else's rights.

A female, according to this theory, may or may not report the offender, depending on the individual and his particular circumstances. She would be concerned that the person might feel shamed and alienated after being reported, or might react in a rebellious manner that would have longterm negative effects on himself and his community. If she knew him, she might talk to him herself, keeping in mind his feelings and how this would affect their relationship, his relationship to his family and friends, his self-esteem, and his physical and emotional health. If she felt that the particular people on the Assembly were better able to handle this person or situation, she might consult them, possibly after discussing this with the individual himself.

In this situation, the male would emphasize individual rights, logic, procedures, and principles of right and wrong; the female would emphasize relationships, caring, individual needs, and the specific situation. Both within this society, and within the Bahá'í community, it is the former approach—or the male ethic—which has official sanction and has been considered morally superior.

Among the many theories seeking to explain differences of values between men and women, one credits them to the process of early gender identification that takes place within infants and children. This theory suggests essentially that girls identify with their mothers to form their self-concept, while boys need to separate themselves from their mother to form theirs. According to this theory, female values reflect a need for attachment and male values reflect a need for separation.[18] Those attitudes expressing intimacy, interdependence, and group harmony would be strongly held by women, and those expressing independence and individuation would be held by men. Conversely, each would be threatened by what is the core of the other's identity.[19]

These strong differences might be altered in a society where the roles and traits of men and women are more evenly balanced, and where men share the caretaking of young children. But, according to Eakins, whatever the source of these male-female differences, there is "no evidence that either men or women are biologically better suited for either an expressive, stroking role, or an instrumental, task-oriented one."[20]

Inequality of Power. A number of feminist writers assert that the differences in male and female personality traits are not so much characteristic of sexual roles and styles per se, as they are characteristic of the traits that two groups of people will display in any unequal relationship: child to parent, subordinate to boss, slave to master. Subservient behavior might include excessive smiling, dependency, passivity, receptivity, and the desire to serve and to please. Hoagland even suggests that many of these traits, including seeming irrationality, are actually attempts at resisting domination.[21]

Cross-cultural studies of gender relationships show that inequality is universal. That is, men are always regarded as the center of cultural value, and their activities are always regarded as more important than those of women.[22] For example, in parts of New Guinea where women grow sweet potatoes and men grow yams, two virtually identical crops, yams are considered the more important food.[23] Regardless of how equal men and women are in a society, Rosaldo observes, "some area of activity is always seen as exclusively or predominantly male, and therefore overwhelmingly and morally important."[24] In our own Bahá'í community, for example, the exclusive right of men to serve on the Universal House of Justice might be viewed by observers as just such an activity.

'Abdu'l-Bahá has stated that men in the past ruled over women by force. Nancy Henley confirms this statement in her study of the politics of communication: "the ultimate underpinning of power is force."[25] Even in the female-dominant society studied by Mead, men ultimately resorted to beating women when they felt shamed by them.[26]

Where actual force is not used, the threat of force may be sufficient. For example, nonverbal behavior studies indicate that staring, towering over, raising one's voice, and even touching may be used to carry the threat of force.[27] Indeed, logic itself has been used as a weapon of power:

In masculine hands logic is often a form of violence, a sly kind of tyranny; the husband, if older and better educated than his wife, assumes on the basis of this superiority to give no weight at all to her opinions when he does not share them; he tirelessly *proves* to her that he is right —Simone de Beauvoir.[28]

Henley asserts that these small gestures of daily communication are really micropolitical acts that support, and are an integral part of, a system that fosters and justifies inequality.[29] She believes that traditional differences in gender styles are actually traceable to differences in power, and are learned rather than innate.[30] For example, personal use of territory is one of the behaviors found to reflect dominance and inequality of power in both animal and human studies. Women consistently have less personal and office space than men, yield their space more to others, and have their space violated more than do men.[31] Further, all other aspects of status being equal, men will receive preferred space.[32] In many homes, for example, it is the husband who has a personal den or office. The wife, who has no room of her own, is also subject to interruptions and requests from both her children and husband on a near twenty-four-hour basis.

Women are also less mobile than men, controlling less personal space. Women traveling alone or frequenting public places such as nightclubs or parks, particularly after dark, are subjected to social disapproval as well as male violence. These male-female differences in the use of space mirror the findings of animal and human dominance which show that subordinates have less control over territory than those in superior positions.[33]

The Women's Movement of the 1960s. Betty Friedan's book, *The Feminine Mystique*, which addresses the psychological oppression of women of her generation, came at the beginning of a resurgence of feminism in the United States in the 1960s.[34] Women at that time were participating in civil rights groups and student, new-left organizations, such as Students for a Democratic Society. The women's movement grew out of their work with these groups, not so much as an extension of their efforts there as a reaction to the oppression they experienced from their new-left brothers.[35]

The position they had in these organizations was much like the position women held in society as a whole—"important but invisible."[36] The writing and position-formulating was done mainly by the men, and the support work of secretary and housekeeper was done by the women.[37] Decisions were made in informal male groups beyond the reach of women. At Harvard, for example, men convened at night in the all-male dormitory and the campus newspaper announced their decisions in the morning.[38] The new-left student groups were designed along male value and social structures, were highly competitive and intellectual, and emphasized the value of verbal and political skills.[39] Despite their egalitarian attitude towards minority groups and oppressed lower classes, they largely ignored women and their oppression.[40]

What made this a particularly sour experience for these women was that these liberal groups espoused an ideology of participatory democracy, equality, and openness.[41] While women were on occasion openly referred to in denigrating terms, such as "dumb chick," for the most part the subservient role women held was unconsciously created, a result of long-standing behaviors and attitudes reflective of society as a whole.[42]

These women decided to form their own movement, one in which they could define their own issues and enjoy the opportunity to experience decision-making and leadership. As the women's movement emerged out of the new left and civil rights groups of the 1960s, it modelled itself after black power groups, by defining issues in women's own terms rather than those of men.[43]

Both women and blacks have filled supportive and inferior roles in a society based on white male standards and institutions. White men viewed both women and blacks as having little individual identity apart from their assigned roles in a white man's society.[44] Both women and blacks learned to "read" their superiors and adopted behaviors and attitudes that reflected their subordinate positions.[45] Women and blacks, therefore, learned to be more sensitive than most men to subtle nonverbal cues of approval or disapproval, much as an office subordinate monitors his boss's moods before approaching him with a question.[46]

When blacks began to raise their position in society, they first adopted white male standards.[47] It was the black power movement that eventually established separate standards for blacks, ones that represented their own strengths and virtues.[48] Women, following suit, created a women's

movement based on female values and virtues. While forming their separate movements, however, both blacks and
women still faced the reality that they lived in a society in
which they intermingle with and are subservient to white
men.

As these liberal groups found out, it is not enough simply
to state a belief in equality. The present system of inequality is based on a complex set of power relations which manifest themselves even at the microlevel of communication
and social relationship. The women's experience in the Bahá'í study class described in the Introduction to this book
parallels that of the women in these new-left groups. By
forming separate women's groups within the Bahá'í community, women can practice leadership, develop self-confidence, and explore issues of concern to them as a group.
However, this cannot be regarded as a permanent alternative or substitute for projects and social action involving
both sexes.

The issue of inequality cannot be resolved merely by
keeping men and women apart. Both must confront the attitudes and behaviors that have kept men in a position of
power and control over women. And this must eventually
be done in a context that includes both sexes. Otherwise,
there will inevitably result a struggle for power between
men and women. Armstrong-Ingram's essay in this volume
documents just such a struggle between all-male and all-
female groups in the early Chicago Bahá'í community.
Women's groups eventually became a means for both
sexes to avoid gender issues, and for men to retain control
of power within the community.

Women's Self-Image. Women have been defined by their
relationships to men and derive their self-image and sense
of self-worth from how they appear to others, rather than
from an independent sense of self.[49] A man is a farmer, a
scholar, or a gentleman, and a woman is his mother, wife,
or daughter.

Woman's identity is often defined by how she relates to a particular man, not by her own achievments or even her own separate identity as an individual. She derives much of her status from her husband's or father's status, and not from her own efforts or place in society. Young girls are often taught to aim high, to marry the president of the company, although their actual role in their husband's life may not be much different from that of the wife of the bookkeeper. Much of this gaining of a sense of self through attachment to another is beginning to change, but it would still be considered a source of shame for most women executives to marry a grocery clerk. Their sense of self-worth and their status in the eyes of others might be significantly lowered.

A woman is taught that taking care of others is her primary role, and thus she has developed a less autonomous self than have most men.[50] Her difficulty with developing herself as an independent individual arises both from her early identification with her mother, as well as from the continuing emphasis on nurturing and maintaining relationships.[51]

Women judge themselves according to their ability to care, to relate to others, and to be supportive and self-sacrificing.[52] This may truly represent an alternative value system, or it may be only a rationalization for the position they have long held within a male-dominated society.[53] Women's position as nurturers may be biologically based and cultivated in society as a necessity for the well-being and development of children. However, this position may also have resulted from the lack of opportunity to hold positions of authority within society.

If, for example, a particular group of people hold major positions of power and make use of other groups as support or service personnel, giving them no opportunity to do otherwise, not only do these support groups develop support skills by practice and necessity, they may even believe the value of service to be superior to that of power, as a compensation for their subordinate position. Women in the Bahá'í Faith are often told that they are superior to men because of these nurturing qualities. Does such praise also function to make these women content with their secondary position within the community?

Given that society views male behavior as the norm, male traits are used as the standard by which all in society are eventually judged.[54] Males tend to devalue women's caretaking because they value personal achievement among themselves.[55] When a man does focus on personal relationships, others consider him to be weak.[56]

Women have not generally adopted the prerequisites to success in the male hierarchical system.[57] They fear they would lose what status and position they now have as wives and mothers if they were to be successful.[58] They also experience anxiety when they become successful and must sacrifice their primary values, particularly those of cooperation and nurturance.[59] Trained from infancy to be indirect, polite, and deferential; they have difficulty wielding direct formal power and displaying aggression.[60] They experience a conflict of values and behavior, as well as role and status conflict—the well-known fear (and reality) for many women is that they must choose between career and family.

Women generally lack the self-confidence that comes from possessing independent status, recognition, and power.[61] Though women may acquire status through their husband or through physical beauty, they do not generally acquire the same power a man would.[62] Women with expertise are still devalued by the belief that only men can be experts.[63] And being male in itself carries higher status.[64]

Because of the supportive role they play in society, women have become passive, dependent, and limited in their individual development.[65] They are subject to psychological depression leading to physical and mental illness. Without a personal sense of identity, they feel bored, insecure, trapped, limited, and often worthless.[66]

'Abdu'l-Bahá Himself has stated that depression in

women can be caused by continued assumptions of male superiority and lack of confidence in her ability to achieve.[67] He has praised women for their accomplishments and traditional qualities and encouraged them to continue to develop through education and effort to acquire abilities and positions formerly assumed by men. He says special attention should be paid to this matter, and that it is more important to educate women than men.[68] He asks that men regard women as equals, and so give them the self-assurance and courage they need to take their rightful place in society.[69]

Nonverbal Behavior. Communication styles, verbal and nonverbal, reflect both the value and the power differences between men and women. We may be unaware of the influence and role that nonverbal behavior plays in conveying messages, as it tends to operate out of our conscious awareness.[70] Nonverbal behavior has an important role in displaying power, as it can be verbally denied, thus enabling a person or group to exert control more easily.[71] In the male-female dance of dominance and submission, the male may display a number of signals in his voice or posture that demand compliance. If the female does not react appropriately, for example, by smiling or speaking softly, the man may eventually react violently.[72] Wife- and child-beating is a common occurrence, one that has often been justified as a necessary means for men to keep order and control within the household.

As mentioned earlier, women are generally more sensitive to nonverbal signals than are men, a skill also ascribed to other subordinate groups, such as blacks in relationship to whites.[73] Generally, the less powerful group knows the more powerful one better than vice versa.[74] They use this sensitivity to obtain the feedback necessary to their survival in a world where force is still a major underpinning of power.[75]

Women look for signs of approval and disapproval from

others. They look for these in eye gaze, body tension, tone and intensity of voice. In addition, they are sensitive to cues of possible threat in physical nearness, direction and intensity of glance and body motion. In Iran, when I walked on the streets of Tehran, I learned to modify my behavior and to monitor the behavior of every man within a certain distance. I walked briskly, maintaining a business-like hold on the way my own body moved, keeping my eyes scanning, but without looking specifically at any one person. Since "accidental" touching and bumping was common, when a man walked toward me on the same sidewalk, I had to judge how close he would be to me when we passed each other. I then subtly altered my direction, so that when we passed we would be far enough apart that it would appear to be a purposeful act were he to bump into me or touch me. I simply learned, as the Persian women did, how to avoid these situations altogether.

The same issues exist in this country, but on a much more dangerous level. Here women's subtle monitoring and assessments must be used, not just to avoid unwanted touching and fondling, but to save our lives. When I go to a public park, I have to carefully consider the time of day, whether to sit on a park bench, whether to smile or respond to a greeting from a man, and whether to linger or walk briskly. I have to be concerned that I may appear too vulnerable or open, and I must be automatically aware of the activities, the body and eye signals of the men within my range of sight. Women constantly monitor the behavior of others in their family, on their jobs, and in the community —always aware of power differences, of being dependent on male favor and approval, and ultimately seeking to diffuse or avoid any overt violence.

Female Communication Style. Women's speech reflects their values, self-image, and position in society. The key word in female communication style is *cooperation*.[76]

Women stress getting along with others, interpersonal exploration, fairness, and sharing.[77]

Within all-female groups, women cooperate, taking turns both in speaking and leadership on an egalitarian basis.[78] In their discussions, they are likely to be personal and to talk about human relationships.[79] In their actual speech style, they tend to express feelings and are sensitive to social cues, such as facial expressions.[80] They are polite and indirect, using implication, qualifiers, and softening devices. A woman might say, "You're coming to my party, aren't you?" using the tagged-on question to soften the preceding statement. She may also modify statements by adding such phrases as "I think" or "I really don't know, but it seems to me . . ." And rather than directly order a subordinate to perform an errand, she might suggest this in an indirect manner: "It would be nice if we had some coffee for this morning's meeting."[81] In all-female communication, there is a shared style and the ease of communication that comes from talking with a person from one's own culture.[82]

A common stereotype of women is that they spend most of their time talking and that they talk more than men do. This has developed, in part, as a result of men measuring women's behavior against the expectation that they should be silent.[83] Another factor in creating this stereotype is that we often see what we expect, screening out what does not fit our preconceptions. A recent classroom study illustrated that, while observers rated girls as talking more than boys in a classroom situation, films of the class revealed that boys actually talked three times more than girls.[84]

Male Communication Style. The key concept in the male communication style is *competition*.[85] Male communication patterns are designed to promote the individual speaker, who vies with others in placing himself in the most prominent position possible within the male hierarchy.[86] Men view competition in speaking as a sport or a game, where each player practices and develops skills to achieve victory.[87] They feel that this competition provides both players with the most effective means of self-improvement.

Male speech patterns emphasize the abstract and stress the external and literal.[88] A man might typically talk about how the equality of the sexes might affect long-range economic productivity in Third-World natons, where a woman might typically ask how this equality would affect decision-making in her family. Men use specialized professional or technical language that demands verifiable proof.[89] Expression of feelings or impressions without either logical or objective evidence is rejected. The male response to a woman's statement like, "the committee dismissed my petition in an offhand manner," would be to challenge: "How do you know that? What did they say?" While a woman's response would be to sympathize: "They did? How awful! How do you feel?" In contrast to the female's nonassertive style, males tend to be louder and more assertive in their speech, directing their attention toward winning an argument.[90]

In all-male groups, men are more likely to talk about themselves than are women in all-female groups.[91] Men usually talk about themselves to show superiority or aggression, while women normally mention themselves to share an emotional reaction to what has been said. Steinem quotes Phil Donahue, the well-known television interviewer, who summarizes this difference:

If you're in a social situation, and women are talking to each other, and one woman says, "I was hit by a car today," all the other women will say, "You're kidding! What happened? Where? Are you all right?" In the same situation with males, one male says, "I was hit by a car today." I guarantee you that there will be another male in the group who will say, "Wait till I tell you what happened to *me*."[92]

Mixed Sex Communication. Most women are not comfortable with the argumentative and competitive style of men.[93] Further, women who do excel at this style risk losing social approval.[94] Women generally are more comfortable talking with other women, sharing their communication styles and common experience.[95]

Men talk more than women in mixed group settings, and tend to dominate and control topics.[96] They do this by a number of communicative devices, particularly by interrupting. Normal turn-taking in conversation is regulated by such behaviors as eye movement, vocalizations, and head nods. Interruptions of this turn-taking process reflect and assert power differences.[97] Studies indicate that "men interrupt women more often than they interrupt other men and that they do so more often than women interrupt either men or other women."[98]

A sample of male-female dialogue is given in this hypothetical discussion of attendance at the Nineteen-Day Feast by John, Susan, Fred, and Mary:

Fred: Let's get started. First, we'll list the points we've covered at the meeting and go from there.

Mary: It seems to me everyone would like to get to know each other, (Fred interrupts here) don't you think?

Fred: We covered that yesterday. We need some concrete solutions.

John: Attendance at Feast has dropped from 100 to 80 over the last year, along with contributions. We should use the canvassing methods I've developed for my firm. They have an 85% success rate.

Fred: The cost to the Fund from these marketing techniques is too high. The fall recruitment drive I started last year is a hands-on program with guaranteed results at low cost.

Mary: How did the participants feel about it? Was
every . . .
Fred: All right, are there any more suggestions?

In addition, topics introduced by men succeed much
more often than those introduced by women.[99] In a study
by Fishman, topics introduced by men succeeded 96% of
the time, while those introduced by women succeeded 36%
of the time.[100] Both women and men use communicative
patterns that encourage male control of topics. Women
tend to be supportive in their speech, generally drawing
others out. They work harder in conversations to keep
them going, asking questions three times as much as
men.[101] They hesitate and are nonassertive, even self-
disparaging. For example, women request while men command.[102]

Women will listen more while men talk more.[103] In addition, men's silence may not necessarily mean they are
listening, but may indicate that they are rejecting the topic
or issue.[104] In addition to silence, men use minimal or perfunctory response to kill a conversation, for example, using
a pause or "um-humm."[105] The topic then becomes one-
sided, not jointly developed by both people, and eventually
breaks down.[106] In other words, men may effectively ignore those topics in which they have no interest.

Women have a harder time gaining the floor in mixed
groups.[107] Men are more likely to give direct, assertive and
even commanding statements and to take charge of a
group.[108] They use communicative techniques that tend to
dominate: staring, pointing, interrupting, ignoring or
responding minimally, using commands, talking loudly,
and using argumentative language. Their use of professional or abstract language mystifies others. Women tend
to use more concrete and personal language.[109] In addition
to and because of the difficulties imposed by male dominat-
ing strategies, women feel hesitant, shy, and inferior about

speaking in front of men.[110] Both sexes perpetuate unequal communicative relations between men and women that parallel those between superiors and subordinates and between parents and children.[111]

Directions: The Meaning of Equality. Communication studies reveal that there is an asymmetrical power relationship between men and women. We cannot continue to believe that we can have equality by merely stating that we believe in it. Behavior and attitudes need to be truly reflective of this principle.

Safilios-Rothschild describes three models of equality: pluralist, assimilationist, and hybrid.[112] The pluralist model states that each subculture in a society should be valued as it is for its own unique characteristics. These subcultures, however, have developed within a system that is based on inequality. Thus, some or many of the characteristics of these subcultures are actually products of assigned roles and oppression in a system designed to support a dominant elite.[113] The fact that women smile more than do men may not be so much an integral part of their personality as it is an expression of submission and an attempt to please and appease.[114] Both the acquired traits of women and the consequent support position they have held in society give them a certain indirect power, but for the most part they simply perpetuate their roles as subordinates.

Within the Bahá'í community, those who argue that women are better suited to the role of mother and supporter of their husbands subscribe to the pluralist theory. Essentially, they argue that different male and female functions have equal spiritual and social value. They see little need for change in traditional roles, but focus instead on the importance of a change in attitudes.

The assimilationist model also supports the current male-dominated social system by assuming that in order to be equal, women and other minorities must adopt the dominant male value system and assume traditional male roles.[115] In effect, the dominant group retains its superior position and reserves its right to judge the behavior of subordinate groups by its own standards.[116] Since the traditional social system is dependent on using subordinate groups for support services, to press for equality on the basis of assimilation goes against the very grain of the system and fosters its breakdown. The balance of society is disrupted, theoretically leaving no one to supply these nurturing or support services.[117]

Striving for so-called androgyny actually pressures women to become like men, but does not urge men to take on female characteristics, or promote self-actualization for either sex.[118] Assimilation promotes male careers for women and the acquisition of masculine communication skills through, for example, assertiveness training, to prepare them for their new roles.[119]

In the Bahá'í community, the advocates of this view encourage women to become more assertive, to speak out in meetings, and to assume more positions of responsibility and prominence within the community, to take their places alongside men. They emphasize statistics that show the discrepancy between men and women in positions of leadership in the community and work to reconcile these differences. Their focus is on women's development, addressing men primarily to ask for support.

The third model is that of the hybrid society, which suggests the transformation of the entire value base and social structure of society.[120] It implies changes in both men and women, each acquiring traits formerly assigned to the other. In essence it means infusing current social structures with traditionally "feminine" traits of nurturing, caring, and cooperation. It also implies that men need to make greater changes in themselves than do women.[121] The reason for this greater change in the role of men stems from the need to feminize both the existing male-dominated social structure and also the traditional behaviors and attitudes that have characterized male roles.

Within the Bahá'í community, advocates of this position urge men to play an equal role in bringing about equality by working on their own development and examining their own goals and behaviors. They call for cooperation and sharing for both men and women in reducing the dichotomy of power, roles, and behavioral styles that have been adopted in Western society.

Although support for all three models may be found in the Bahá'í writings, the hybrid model of equality best embodies 'Abdu'l-Bahá's well-known assessment of the future balance of masculinity and femininity:

> *Hence the new age will be an age less masculine, and more permeated with the feminine ideals—or, to speak more exactly, will be an age in which the masculine and feminine elements of civilization will be more evenly balanced.*[122]

It calls for a transformation of society and women's and men's place within it.[123] This hybrid model presented by Safilios-Rothschild is essentially the Bahá'í blueprint of a future society based on humanitarian principles, social responsibility, and a more meaningful sense of community.[124]

In this society, men would learn to acquire for themselves patience, cooperation, and intimacy in relationships, and women would become more individuated, assertive, and self-confident. Neither would need to discard the positive traits that were part of their traditional roles.[125] Both could learn these qualities from each other.[126] Androgyny in this context would represent a balancing of male and female qualities within each person, providing for individual and gender differences, but not those based on inequality of power and privilege.[127]

This transformation and reformulation of society and

gender identities is one of great complexity, with ramifications beyond a balance of gender power. 'Abdu'l-Bahá has said that world peace will not come about until women have achieved true equality with men:

> *When all mankind shall receive the same opportunity of education and the equality of men and women be realized, the foundations of war will be utterly destroyed.*[128]

To achieve this equality, 'Abdu'l-Bahá strongly promoted education and encouraged women to enter into all aspects of the public sphere, including politics, science, and art.[129] As De Beauvoir has stated: "Only gainful employment will liberate women from their dependent, relative, submissive status."[130]

I do not take entering the public sphere to mean that women should provide the "nurturing" role within the sphere while the men provide the "leadership." Although some elements of this have and will certainly happen, I feel that the ultimate goal of a Bahá'í society is for both men and women to exhibit leadership and caretaking, not for women to be again compartmentalized into functions based on tradition and male needs.

The peace movement, for example, is thought by some Bahá'ís to be primarily a woman's issue, as she is "peaceful" while men are "warlike." But for the task of peace to be particularly delegated to women is to keep both women and peace as side issues that do not seriously threaten the dominant system of competition and warfare. It is men, as well as women, who need to incorporate peace into their roles and institutions. Without the skills, confidence, and channels necessary for women to fully participate in all aspects of the public sphere, they can have little effect on mainstream attitudes. An all-female peace movement would become, in effect, yet another version of the traditional women's auxiliary, a method of diverting women from positions of prominence and influence within an organization or community (and thus preventing them from really affecting it).[131]

While 'Abdu'l-Bahá admonishes men to change their attitudes toward women, those in power in actuality seldom give it up without a fight.[132] Nor do women want to be "granted" equality, as though it were another privilege for men to bestow. Women need to define their own issues, not have men define issues for them.[133]

Towards a New Model of Communication. Communication between men and women is currently a cross-cultural encounter, with differences in power, styles, and goals. Accomplishing changes in traditional roles and attitudes won't be easy, since each cultural group generally favors itself and its own personal style. Women see themselves, for example, as more cooperative and egalitarian in their conversation styles, drawing out each person and being sensitive to his or her feelings. They see men as just the opposite, as competing and showing off, being insensitive and impolite. Men see themselves as strong, independent, and competent. They view their struggle for dominance as a test of mettle, a honing of skills, and a way of improving the quality of intellectual and practical performance. They see women as pandering to weakness, unwilling to test their strength, and unconcerned with political, social, and economic issues.

In a mixed discussion women's tendency to listen and draw the other out puts them at a disadvantage with men who do not always wait for conversational pauses before jumping in with their own ideas. The question for women is how are they going to deal with this more aggressive style. In mixed-sex communication it is typically the male that dominates the conversation. In order to achieve a balance, men need to learn to listen, to be sensitive to others and develop a spirit of cooperation; women need to develop self-confidence and a willingness to risk speaking their mind.

An examination of the existing communication patterns

in the Bahá'í community will reveal a tendency for men to lead meetings, initiate and control topics, and dominate conversations. Women do much of the actual support work and faithfully keep the social fabric of the community together. These practices are the result of our current beliefs, as well as our upbringing. They reflect the pluralists' inability to face the full implications of keeping women in subordinate positions while maintaining that they are spiritually superior.

The assimilationists among us would have everyone jostling for position to serve in leadership capacities. Women essentially would be expected to speak and act the way men do, with the subtle assumption that men would set the standards and decide whether and when the women were equal. However, this would foster an impossible imbalance in our community, with everyone wanting to speak at meetings and generate ideas, and with few people willing to teach children's classes, serve tea, take minutes, or type correspondence.

Only when both men and women are fully able to value and adopt the positive qualities of masculinity and femininity as human virtues will the community be able to realize the spiritual ideals of a Bahá'í society. Only then will the concepts of masculinity and femininity no longer stand as barriers impeding the gradual unfoldment of equality within Bahá'í family and community life.

Notes

1. Chodorow, "Being and Doing," pp. 173–74.
2. Mead, *Male and Female*, p. 16.
3. Mead, *Sex and Temperament*.
4. Frieze et al., *Women and Sex Roles*, p. 53.
5. Ibid., pp. 81–82.

6. Rosaldo, "Women, Culture, and Society," p. 30.

7. Parlee, "Deal Me In," p. 14; Steinem, *Outrageous Acts*, p. 183; Rosaldo, "Women, Culture, and Society," p. 29.

8. Ibid., p. 30.

9. Ibid., pp. 29, 42; Rosaldo and Lamphere, "Introduction," p. 7.

10. Toffler, *The Third Wave*, pp. 42–44, 49.

11. Adler, "Women as Androgynous Managers," pp. 418–19.

12. Toffler, *The Third Wave*, p. 209; Whitehurst, *Women in America*, p. 15.

13. Whitehurst, *Women in America*, p. 15.

14. Eakins and Eakins, *Sex Differences*, p. 19.

15. Battle-Sister, "Conjectures," p. 416.

16. Gilligan, *Different Voice*, pp. 16–17; Eakins and Eakins, *Sex Differences*, p. 19.

17. Gilligan, *Different Voice*, pp. 1, 19, 22.

18. Ibid., p. 171.

19. Ibid., pp. 8, 17.

20. Eakins and Eakins, *Sex Differences*, p. 79.

21. Hoagland, "'Femininity,'" pp. 90–91.

22. Rosaldo, "Woman, Culture, and Society," pp. 19–20; Rosaldo and Lamphere, "Introduction," p. 2; Frieze et al., *Women and Sex Roles*, p. 80.

23. Rosaldo, "Woman, Culture, and Society," p. 19.

24. Ibid., p. 20.

25. Women: #25, p. 13; Henley, *Body Politics*, p. 189.

26. Mead, *Sex and Temperament*, p. 263.

27. Henley, *Body Politics*, p. 183.

28. Battle-Sister, "Conjectures," p. 418.

29. Henley, *Body Politics*, p. 179.

30. Ibid., p. 2.

31. Ibid., p. 39; Safilios-Rothschild, *Toward a Sociology*, p. 41.

32. Henley, *Body Politics*, p. 37.

33. Ibid., p. 36

34. Steinem, *Outrageous Acts*, p. 215.

35. Evans, *Personal Politics*, pp. 212–13.

36. Ibid., p. 111.

37. Ibid., pp. 108, 213; Schwarzer, *After the Second Sex*, pp. 32–33.

38. Evans, *Personal Politics*, p. 116.

39. Ibid., pp. 108–09, 112–13.

40. Ibid., pp. 116, 212–13.

41. Ibid., pp. 108, 213.

42. Ibid., pp. 109, 213; Schwarzer, *After the Second Sex*, p. 33.

43. Evans, *Personal Politics*, p. 200.

44. Kochman, *Black and White Styles*, p. 8.

45. Steinem, "The Politics of Talking," p. 86; Blassingame, *The Slave Community*, p. 200.

46. Eakins and Eakins, *Sex Differences*, pp. 149–50.

47. Frazier, *Black Bourgeoisie*, pp. 146–49; Coombs, "Booker T. Washington," pp. 123–31.

48. "Martin Luther King Writes," p. 41; Cortés et al., *Three Perspectives*, p. 311; Killens, "Explanation," p. 315.

49. De Beauvoir, *The Second Sex*, p. xix; Eakins and Eakins, *Sex Differences*, p. 53; Whitehurst, *Women in America*, p. 109.

50. Gilligan, *Different Voice*, pp. 7–8.

51. Ibid., p. 7.

52. Ibid., p. 17; Whitehurst, *Women in America*, p. 98.

53. Whitehurst, *Women in America*, p. 98.

54. Gilligan, *Different Voice*, p. 14; Eakins and Eakins, *Sex Differences*, p. 38.

55. Gilligan, *Different Voice*, p. 17.

56. Ibid., p. 17.

57. Bernard, *Women, Wives, Mothers*, p. 11.

58. Whitehurst, *Women in America*, p. 125.

59. Gilligan, *Different Voice*, p. 15.

60. Frieze et al., *Women and Sex Roles*, pp. 54, 308; Matthiasson, "Conclusion," p. 423.

61. Frieze et al., *Women and Sex Roles*, pp. 304–08.

62. Parlee, "Deal Me In," p. 305.

63. Frieze et al., *Women and Sex Roles*, p. 307.

64. Ibid., p. 305.

65. Whitehurst, *Women in America*, p. 126.

66. Ibid., pp. 119–20, 126.

67. Women: #104, p. 52.

68. Women: #24, p. 13.

69. Women: #104, p. 52.

70. Soucie, "Common Misconceptions," p. 209.

71. Parlee, "Conversational Politics," p. 55.

72. Battle-Sister, "Conjectures," p. 418.

73. Henley, *Body Politics*, p. 13; Blassingame, *Slave Community*, p. 200.

74. Steinem, *Outrageous Acts*, p. 185; Steinem, "Politics of Talking," p. 86.

75. Blassingame, *Slave Community*, p. 200; Eisenberg and Smith, *Nonverbal Communication*, pp. 93–94; Steinem, *Outrageous Acts*, p. 185.

76. Steinem, *Outrageous Acts*, p. 183; Gilligan, *Different Voice*, pp. 10–11; Parlee, "Deal Me In," p. 14.

77. Eakins and Eakins, *Sex Differences*, pp. 38, 51.

78. Steinem, *Outrageous Acts*, p. 183; Parlee, "Deal Me In," p. 14.

79. Gilligan, *Different Voice*, p. 16; Steinem, *Outrageous Acts*, p. 182.

80. Eakins and Eakins, *Sex Differences*, p. 149.

81. Ibid., pp. 41–48.

82. Steinem, *Outrageous Acts*, p. 156; idem, "Politics of Talking," p. 86.

83. Steinem, "Politics of Talking," p. 45.

84. Sadker, "Sexism in the Schoolroom," p. 54.

85. Eakins and Eakins, *Sex Differences*, p. 51; Gilligan, *Different Voice*, pp. 10–11; Parlee, "Conversational Politics," p. 14; Ehrenreich, "Talking in Couples," p. 36.

86. Steinem, *Outrageous Acts*, p. 183; Eakins and Eakins, *Sex Differences*, p. 38.

87. Ehrenreich, "Talking in Couples," p. 36.

88. Steinem, *Outrageous Acts*, p. 183.

89. Battle-Sister, "Conjectures," p. 418; Eakins and Eakins, *Sex Differences*, pp. 48–49.

90. Eakins and Eakins, *Sex Differences*, pp. 48, 51, 105.

91. Steinem, *Outrageous Acts*, p. 182; Steinem, "Politics of Talking," p. 84.

92. Steinem, *Outrageous Acts*, p. 182.

93. Eakins and Eakins, *Sex Differences*, p. 49.

94. Ibid., p. 52.

95. Steinem, "Politics of Talking," p. 86.

96. Steinem, *Outrageous Acts*, pp. 178–79; Schwarzer, *After the Second Sex*, p. 34; Henley, *Body Politics*, p. 74; Sadker, "Sexism in the Schoolroom," p. 54.

97. Parlee, "Conversational Politics," p. 52.

98. Ehrenreich, "Talking in Couples," p. 48; Henley, *Body Politics*, p. 74; Parlee, "Conversational Politics," p. 52.

99. Steinem, *Outrageous Acts*, p. 182.

100. Ehrenreich, "Talking in Couples," p. 48; Parlee, "Conversational Politics," p. 55.

101. Parlee, "Conversational Politics," p. 55.

102. Henley, *Body Politics*, pp. 77–78.

103. Steinem, *Outrageous Acts*, p. 178; Henley, *Body Politics*, p. 74.

104. Steinem, *Outrageous Acts*, p. 179.

105. Parlee, "Conversational Politics," p. 56.

106. Ibid., p. 55.

107. Henley, *Body Politics*, p. 74.

108. Schwarzer, *After the Second Sex*, p. 34; Henley, *Body Politics*, p. 77; Steinem, *Outrageous Acts*, p. 179.

109. Steinem, *Outrageous Acts*, p. 179; Battle-Sister, "Conjectures," p. 418; Gilligan, *Different Voice*, p. 16.

110. Schwarzer, *After the Second Sex*, p. 34.

111. Eakins and Eakins, *Sex Differences*, p. 176; Parlee, "Conversational Politics," p. 52.

112. Safilios-Rothschild, *Toward a Sociology*, p. 348.

113. Schwarzer, *After the Second Sex*, p. 78; Safilios-Rothschild, *Toward a Sociology*, p. 349.

114. Eakins and Eakins, *Sex Differences*, pp. 155–59.

115. Safilios-Rothschild, *Toward a Sociology*, pp. 351, 353.

116. Ibid., p. 353; Allport, *Nature of Prejudice*, p. 39.

117. Safilios-Rothschild, *Toward a Sociology*, p. 351.

118. Steinem, *Outrageous Acts*, p. 158.

119. Safilios-Rothschild, *Toward a Sociology*, p. 353; Steinem, *Outrageous Acts*, p. 177.

120. Whitehurst, *Women in America*, p. 101; Safilios-Rothschild, *Toward a Sociology*, p. 353.

121. Safilios-Rothschild, *Toward a Sociology*, p. 352.

122. Women: #25, p. 13.

123. Schwarzer, *After the Second Sex*, p. 116.

124. Safilios-Rothschild, *Toward a Sociology*, p. 352.

125. Bernard, *Women, Wives, Mothers*, p. 27.
126. Schwarzer, *After the Second Sex*, p. 78; Steinem, *Outrageous Acts*, p. 175.
127. Mandle, *Women and Social Change*, p. 187.
128. Women: #82, p. 38.
129. Women: #23, pp. 11–12; #106, p. 53.
130. De Beauvoir, *The Second Sex*, p. 755.
131. Safilios-Rothschild, *Toward a Sociology*, p. 352.
132. Goldenberg, *Oppression*, p. 24; Bernard, *Women, Wives, Mothers*, p. 24.
133. Schwarzer, *After the Second Sex*, p. 35.

Bibliography

Adler, Nancy. "Women As Androgynous Managers: A Conceptualization of the Potential for American Women in International Management." *International Journal of Intercultural Relations.* Vol. 3 (1979) pp. 407–436.

Allport, Gordon. *The Nature of Prejudice.* Reading, Mass.: Addison-Wesley Publishing Company, 1979.

Battle-Sister, Ann. "Conjectures on the Female Culture Question." *Journal of Marriage and The Family (Special Issue: Sexism in Family Studies?)* Vol. 33, No. 3 (February 1971) pp. 411–20.

Bernard, Jessie. *Women, Wives, Mothers: Values and Options.* Chicago: Aldine Publishing Co., 1975.

Blassingame, John W. *The Slave Community: Plantation Life in the Antebellum South.* New York: Oxford University Press, 1971.

Chodorow, Nancy. "Being and Doing: A Cross-Cultural Examination of the Socialization of Males and Females." In *Woman in Sexist Society: Studies in Power and Powerlessness*, ed. by Vivian Gornick and Barbara K. Moran, pp. 173–97. New York: Basic Books, Inc., 1971.

Coombs, Norman. *The Black Experience in America.* New York: Twayne Publications, Inc., 1972.

Cortés, Carlos E.; Ginsburg, Arlin I.; Green, Alan W. F.; Joseph,

James A. *Three Perspectives in Ethnicity: Blacks, Chicanos and Native Americans.* New York: G. P. Putnam's, 1976.

De Beauvoir, Simone. *The Second Sex.* New York: Vintage Books, 1952.

Eakins, Barbara Westbrook and Eakins, R. Gene. *Sex Differences in Human Communication.* Boston: Houghton Mifflin Company, 1978.

Ehrenreich, Barbara. "The Politics of Talking in Couples," *Ms.* Vol. 9, No. 11 (May 1981) pp. 46–48.

Eisenberg, Abne M. and Smith, Ralph R., Jr. *Nonverbal Communication.* Indianapolis: The Bobbs-Merrill Company, Inc., 1971.

Evans, Sara. *Personal Politics: The Roots of Women's Liberation in the Civil Rights Movement and the New Left.* New York: Alfred A. Knopf, 1979.

Frazier, E. Franklin. *Black Bourgeoisie: The Rise of a New Middle Class.* New York: The Free Press, 1957.

Friedan, Betty. *The Feminine Mystique.* New York: Dell Publishing Co., 1963.

Frieze, Irene H.; Parsons, Jacquelynne E.; Ruble, Diane N.; Zellman, Gail L. *Women and Sex Roles: A Social Psychological Perspective.* New York: W. W. Norton and Company, 1978.

Gilligan, Carol. *In a Different Voice.* Cambridge, Mass.: Harvard Univ. Press, 1982.

Goldenberg, I. Ira. *Oppression and Social Intervention.* Chicago: Nelson-Hall, 1978.

Henley, Nancy M. *Body Politics: Power, Sex, and Nonverbal Communication.* Englewood Cliffs, N.J.: Prentice-Hall, Inc., 1977.

Hoagland, Sarah Lucia. "'Femininity,' Resistance, and Sabotage." In *"Femininity," "Masculinity," and Androgyny: A Modern Philosophical Discussion,* ed. by Mary Vetterling-Braggin. Totowa, N.J.: Rowman and Allanheld Publishers, 1982.

Hyman, Herbert H. "The Value Systems of Different Classes: A Social Psychological Contribution to the Analysis of Stratification." In *Class, Status and Power: A Reader in Social Stratification,* ed. by Reinhard Bendix and Seymour Martin Lipset, pp. 426–42. Glencoe, Ill.: The Free Press, 1953.

Killens, John Oliver. "Explanation of the 'Black Psyche.'" In

Three Perspectives in Ethnicity: Blacks, Chicanos, and Native Americans, ed. by Carlos E. Cortés et al., pp. 311–319. New York: G. P. Putnam's, 1976.

Kochman, Thomas. *Black and White Styles in Conflict*. Chicago: Univ. of Chicago Press, 1981.

Mandle, Joan D. *Women and Social Change in America*. Princeton, N.J.: Princeton Book Company, 1979.

"Martin Luther King, Jr., Writes About the Birth of the Black Power Slogan." In *The Rhetoric of Black Power*, ed. by Scott, Robert L. and Brockriede, Wayne, pp. 25–64. New York: Harper and Row, 1969.

Matthiasson, Carolyn J. *Many Sisters: Women in Cross-Cultural Perspective*. New York: The Free Press, 1974.

Mead, Margaret. *Male and Female: A Study of the Sexes in a Changing World*. New York: Mentor Books, 1955.

———. *Sex and Temperament in Three Primitive Societies*. New York: Morrow Quill Paperbacks, 1963.

Parlee, Mary. "Deal Me In: Why Women Should Play Poker." *Ms.*, Vol. 13, No. 7 (January 1985) pp. 14–15.

———. "Conversational Politics." *Psychology Today*, Vol. 12 (May 1979) pp. 48–9, 51–2, 55–6.

Rosaldo, Michelle Zimbalist. "Woman, Culture, and Society: A Theoretical Overview." In *Woman, Culture, and Society*, ed. by Michelle Zimbalist Rosaldo and Louise Lamphere, pp. 17–42. Stanford, Calif.: Stanford Univ. Press, 1974.

Rosaldo, Michelle Zimbalist and Lamphere, Louise. "Introduction." In *Woman, Culture, and Society*, ed. by Michelle Zimbalist Rosaldo and Louise Lamphere, pp. 6–15. Stanford, Calif.: Stanford University Press, 1974.

Sadker, Myra and Sadker, David. "Sexism in the Schoolroom of the '80's." *Psychology Today*, Vol. 19, No. 3 (March 1985) pp. 54–57.

Saffioti, Heleieth I. B. *Women in Class Society*. New York: Monthly Review Press, 1978.

Safilios-Rothschild, Constantina. *Toward a Sociology of Women*. Lexington, Mass.: Xerox College Publishing, 1972.

Schwarzer, Alice. *After the Second Sex: Conversations with Simone de Beauvoir*. New York: Pantheon Books, 1984.

Soucie, Robert M. "Common Misconceptions About Nonverbal

Communication." In *Nonverbal Behavior: Applications and Cultural Implications*, ed. by Aaron Wolfgang, pp. 209–18. New York: Academic Press, 1979.

Steinem, Gloria. *Outrageous Acts and Everyday Rebellions.* New York: Holt, Rinehart and Winston, 1983.

———. "The Politics of Talking in Groups." *Ms.*, Vol. 9, No. 11 (May 1981) pp. 43, 45, 84, 86–89.

Toffler, Alvin. *The Third Wave.* New York: Bantam Books, 1980.

Whitehurst, Carol A. *Women in America: The Oppressed Majority.* Santa Monica, Calif.: Goodyear Publishing Co., Inc., 1977.

Women: Extracts from the Writings of Bahá'u'lláh, 'Abdu'l-Bahá, Shoghi Effendi and the Universal House of Justice. Comp. by the Research Department of the Universal House of Justice. Ontario, Canada: Bahá'í Canada Publications, 1986.

Breakin' into the Boys Club

by Muhtadia Rice

IT WAS 1972. *Ms.* magazine was preparing its introductory issue. The Watergate break-in was America's newest crisis. The Vietnam War continued to traumatize the nation. Out of 31 million American women: 6.7 million did not work outside the home, 24 million were working in low-paying clerical, service, or factory jobs, and fewer than 300,000 were in the professional ranks. The word career was not a part of the female vocabulary.

Along with millions of other youth, I was caught up in the passion of the late 60s. Like most "hippies," "radicals," "militants," and "rebels," I passionately wanted to end the war and reform America. I had become a Bahá'í as a youth in 1968. I was attracted to the social teachings of the Faith: the equality of men and women, elimination of prejudices, the oneness of mankind, and universal peace—beliefs that I had embraced years earlier. The spiritual aspects of the Bahá'í Faith would not become realities for me until much later. As a Bahá'í youth I was willing to put myself on the line to work, and to fight if need be, for my social commitments and beliefs.

I spent 1968 and 1969 as a VISTA volunteer in the slums of Chicago and Cleveland. VISTA (Volunteers In Service

155

To America) was instituted by President Kennedy as a national program to combat poverty in the United States. My two years in the corps were spent organizing and protesting. We coordinated groups for welfare rights organizations, developed rehabilitation programs for the retarded, promoted Black History courses in the local housing project, helped launch Head Start programs, counseled Puerto Rican youth gangs—all while living in the local settlement house. These were the safer aspects of the job. I also participated in farm worker strikes, boycotted A & P markets, led sit-ins, and repeatedly ended up in the Cleveland jail. I was active in the church sanctuary movement that gave refuge to Canada-bound draft evaders. I led boycotts against diamonds from South Africa, and head lettuce from the U.S. and Mexico. I marched by day and in candlelight as well. These were years of hazard and risk, but also of excitement and opportunity.

My full-on, radical-60s experience would hardly have seemed to qualify me as the ideal candidate to become a "Fortune 40" corporate sales executive, but that is what happened. My activities during that turbulent decade had not only given me organizational skills, but also competitive skills that would rapidly pay off. Timing and history were ironically on my side.

Major American corporations were coming under pressure from Congress and from the growing women's movement to establish affirmative action programs. The political and social climate of the time demanded that women and minorities be admitted to visible and lucrative professional and management positions. Requiring assistance to do this, the corporations relied on "headhunters," executive recruiters who specialized in finding the right person for the right company.

I was looking for a job, and I met a headhunter. I vividly remember him telling me that he had found "the chance of a lifetime" for me—a position with one of the most prestigious and profitable international companies in business. Only the "cream of the crop" got hired at this top-flight, Fortune 40 corporation. None of that really mattered to me. I just didn't want to get stuck in a dead-end secretarial job. Never again. And, oh yes, more money!

The headhunter rehearsed me for the job interview. If I got the job, I would be the first woman, and the first minority woman, in this particular branch of the firm. Something about being a trailblazer appealed to me. I was a tomboy growing up; I had been among the few women (as barely an adult) in VISTA. I was used to taking risks. Why stop now?

I had no experience in dealing with business professionals. I knew that my radical background, my VISTA experience, my Bahá'í beliefs, and my few secretarial jobs were not going to impress these big corporate men. I figured that I had just better look nice and act like a lady. My complete naiveté saved me from any real expectations—or fears.

I arrived for the interview at 8:00 A.M. amidst a flurry of office people darting about. The switchboard operator was frazzled, the phones were busy and more modern than anything I had seen. A man approached me and introduced himself as the sales manager. He asked me to follow him, and we entered a windowless, almost barren office with only a desk and one large square glass ashtray on it. He instructed me to sit across the desk from him.

With only a long pause and no further instructions, he stared directly at me, head to toe. Suddenly, he broke the silence, pushing the ashtray across the desk. "Sell me this ashtray!" he demanded.

Startled, but even more indignant at this command, I came back with a thoughtless, streetwise reply, "Why should I," I dared him. I slid the ashtray back toward him. "I could sell you the shirt *off* your back." There was silence. I was sure that I had blown the interview and lost any chance for a job. But I had to save face. I held my defiant position and watched his eyes grow bigger. For the next 40 or 50 seconds, an eternity stood still. I put all my will, determination, and sheer ignorance on the line.

"You have balls!" he broke the silence. "My God, you're a woman with balls!" he exclaimed in disbelief.

Now I was really confused. I had no idea what this meant. It sounded dirty to me. Was this guy some kind of wierdo? I didn't know what to say, so I kept quiet. Although this was a rare response for me, it turned out to be highly appropriate. He began orating rapidly about how unusual it was to find a female with natural aggressiveness, fearlessness, and strength. It dawned on me that somewhere along the line I must have said the secret word. Months later I learned that when a salesperson is closing a sale, the one who talks first loses. The sales manager had presumed that I knew what I was doing and was closing him. He never found out that it was simply ignorance on my part, and I certainly never told him. I may have been ignorant, but I wasn't stupid!

That wasn't all. There were ten more interviews, which included such irrelevant, brainless, and illegal questions as: "This is hard work. Aren't you afraid?"; "Are your periods regular?"; "Do you get bad cramps?"; "Do you think you'll be getting married soon?"; "Why do you want a man's job?" A month later, I was hired as a sales representative responsible for selling capital business equipment. I had just turned twenty-four.

As my nine-month sales training began, I was the only woman and one of the youngest peers entering an old, firmly established men's club. I was left to my own limited and immature devices to survive in a foreign and highly alienating environment. I shed my naiveté, layer by layer. I began to recognize my talents—usually only after someone else would tell me about them. Daily I was to become more aware of my personal capabilities. I measured my new skills with tests and other professional yardsticks, but there were only male peers with whom I could compare myself.

My boyfriend at the time told me that I would never succeed. Spurred by his remark, I determined to keep moving forward—and without him! My friends didn't know what capital equipment was, and they couldn't understand why I wanted to sell "big machines." I found my social circle shifting rapidly. I was changing too.

It was sheer survival. Massive amounts of information were being hurled at me in training. I had to understand how ten or fifteen different business machines functioned technically. I had to know how to sell each one of them in different business environments and how to make the most skillful professional presentations. Thinking on your feet took on new meaning. As my mental powers sharpened, I compensated for my sex with cutting wit and a shrewd recognition of the weaknesses of others. Seeming perpetually smart, showing cool confidence, always being correct, and sounding constantly persuasive were mandatory tools of success. Being feminine, acting softly, like a lady, spelled death in these all-male ranks.

My job rapidly became a career. As a fast-track management candidate, I began thinking of my corporate position five years ahead. Among the men, I was either admired or condemned. I was either a comrade or an adversary. Forced to extend their game rules to include a woman for the first time, the men were as unsure of themselves in the new environment as I was. On all-male turf, I was not familiar with the athletic jargon or the common bond of male sexuality.

Reactions of men to me were almost always immediately sexual and inappropriate. I became the object of new sexual jokes, jealous attacks, sexual propositions, and crude cat calls. My sex was noticed first, not my value as a person or my capacity as a business professional. Distracted by the sheer novelty of my sexual presence, I was stared at with perverted fascination, as if I were an alien invader.

One of my customers somehow interpreted my sales pitch as a sexual solicitation. His abrupt and lewd suggestion frightened me. (He requested that I come into his office and take off my panties.) I made a hurried escape and was wary of all sales situations thereafter. Once, when I suspected two businessmen of being less than professional when they asked me to meet them in a nearby hotel for a follow-up sales presentation, I insisted that my boss accompany me. Convinced that I was overreacting, he came along only reluctantly. The hotel room was a suite, with a champagne table in full regalia prominently displayed near the bedroom. No briefcases in sight, it was clear they didn't want a sales talk. They were deservedly embarrassed; my boss was astounded. I was disgusted, and forever more suspicious of men.

A new Don Juan was hired in my branch. He kept himself busy proudly propositioning and bedding most of the secretaries in the office, and the secretaries of his clients. One day, he decided that I should be fair game as well. As I passed his desk one early morning, he grabbed my arms, flipped me on my back, pinned me prone on his desk, and planted one of his juiciest kisses right on my mouth.

Well, I wasn't one of "those" women. I swiftly pulled my knee into his crotch, sprayed his kiss all over his face, and slapped him as hard as I could. Back on my feet in seconds, I attacked him with the foulest words in the English language. I straightened my dress and plowed into the boss's office, demanding that Don Juan be fired on the spot.

My manager slowly began to smirk. There was silence. I could see that he didn't believe me, or he didn't care. The story spread like wildfire in the office. "He was only having fun" was the line. And *I* didn't know how to have fun. I knew I was outnumbered. My hurt and anger overwhelmed me. It was a full three years before Don Juan was finally fired for accosting the secretary of a VIP client.

Of course, my corporate career had its rewards. I managed to break several sales records. Even this, however, was not without sexual incident. The Italian macho stud of the office hurled the public accusation that I had only achieved success by handing out sexual favors to every customer I had. Nobody took him seriously, but I was deeply wounded—almost defeated—by the unfounded attack on my character. Rapidly, I developed thicker skin.

As I interacted with male coworkers, made presentations to male prospects, and sold to male customers, I began to anticipate the inevitable reactions. To them I was a woman, and *only* a woman, by virtue of my sex. I was to be ogled, inspected, and assessed for my face, breasts, legs, hair, and voice. This had to do with sexual availability, but not completely. I could have been ugly, ninety, and dressed in a bag, and they still would have noticed my sex before my professional abilities.

During the sexual/body inventory that went first, the males would tune out the content of our interaction. They were so distracted that they could watch me make motions, and hear sounds from my mouth, but would have no idea what I did or said. Deciding whether or not I should be pursued sexually, they would simply ignore everything else. To be effective, I had to learn to distract these men from this purely carnal, time-wasting, and irrelevant attention and shift the action to my own purpose.

I discovered the key. The more abrasive and the less feminine I acted, the shorter the inventory would last. The more like a man I behaved, the more serious attention was paid to my skills and my product. I used assertive body language, a strong, gripping handshake, deep and commanding vocal intonation, bold vocabulary and jargon, riveting eye contact, and an unwavering aggressive attitude. I learned to skillfully intimidate and to threaten with unrelenting domination. I had the best trainers. I simply mirrored the behavior of my peers.

Eventually, I became "one of the guys." Ironically, from

this closer perspective I also began to appreciate men. There developed an unexpected and fresh sense of camaraderie and fellowship. Even in our competitive position, there grew bonds of partisanship and collaboration. Professional interactions changed previously unfamiliar situations into supportive and cooperative transactions. New ground was trod on both sides.

I had been given a unique opportunity to gain insight into male values and standards and to understand how and why men perceived women as they did. As I shared the male world, I found myself also sharing some of their attitudes. Surrounded by inept, unambitious, trivial, and superficial secretaries, it was easy to relate to feelings of male superiority. The women's behavior was in complete contrast to theirs. Usually, women's contributions to our business were mechanical, appeared minimally important and easily replaceable in the fast business world. Their discussions about nail polish colors, soap operas, fashion, hairdos, children, and their shameless gossip, could easily be dismissed. What we, the men, were doing was important, integral to the company's success, prestigious, and skilled.

The women were excluded from positions of power. They were professionally disenfranchised, and *so* submissive and disinterested. They were incapable of seeing the "bigger picture," lacked business orientation, and were distracted by emotional concerns. Above all, they had no desire to become part of the male world. In that alone, they were inferior.

Most of the women were working to supplement their husband's incomes, some were divorced and on their first jobs, others were single and searching for husbands. Many of them became romantically linked and sexually involved with the men in the office. On rare occasions, a true romance would bud—and on rarer occasions blossom into a short-lived marriage. But the divorce would soon cause one or both parties to change their employment, rather than create post-marital office havoc.

This was the decade of sexual revolution: most women took the position that they could be as sexually free as men. The result was on-going office affairs without limit or regard for marital status. Discretion was not a strong point. On one occasion, I saw one of the sales executives humping a secretary against the wall in the corridor. She, in flattered bliss at snagging the interest of one of the office jocks, was giggling; he, proudly flaunting his latest office conquest, was assured of his sexual prowess.

This body sharing among executives and subordinates had everything to do with the inferior position of women and the value judgments made about them by men. The women felt they were advancing the cause of equality by making themselves sexually available. The men did not. Convinced that they were inferior, the men simply pigeonholed these women as sluts and whores. These constant escapades supported the sexist environment and eventually had a negative impact on me.

For three years I would remain the only woman executive within my all-male branch. I had inadvertently set a standard for women that wasn't being met by other female applicants. I had played the "one-up" game hard and well, becoming more male than the men, driving the best sports cars, being seen in impressive places. My super-woman reputation made comparisons hard. How could any woman coming in match this example?

When the third year had passed and the second woman was finally hired, she failed abominably. She also had an affair with the boss. This was not uncommon, but in the higher ranks, discretion was mandatory. She didn't have it. After her short-lived tenure and premature resignation, it was almost another two years before male management was willing to take a risk on female No. 3. All this made me look all the more honorable, cool, and successful. I had never gotten my nose dirty.

Being a Bahá'í in the corporate environment took some doing. Office parties were always awkward. If I didn't go, I was thought of as a snob. If I did go, I would end up refusing the host's finest alcohol and/or drugs. Since I didn't drink, drug, or sleep around, I just didn't fit in. I was young, single, attractive, exotic, outgoing, even somewhat flamboyant. I had a sense of humor and I loved to dance. Yet socializing was uneasy.

Obvious problems were being a woman, a minority, and athletically disinterested. My moral convictions were perceived as passé. I was outspoken on women's issues, and so was labeled a broken record. I was vocal in protesting corporate and civil racism, unpopular topics back then. Being a Bahá'í just meant I was all the more different. What had made me professionally successful also made me socially unacceptable.

While the corporate world was adjusting to me, the Bahá'í community only barely tolerated my ambitions. There was little support for my corporate identity, my image, or my objectives. Traditionalist Bahá'í women confused my drive with lesbian tendencies. "True Bahá'í women should spend their time caring for their husbands and families," I was told. "Sacrifice is spiritual superiority," they chorused.

Other Bahá'í women were less rigid in their views. Like me, they believed that by entering professional careers we were contributing to the establishment of Bahá'u'lláh's principle of equality for men and women. For us, "having it all" was not only acceptable, but timely and appropriate—especially for Bahá'ís. Unexpectedly, I became the mentor to these women who admired me and supported me and saw me as a role-model for their own career aspirations.

The years that I spent in corporate environs taught me perhaps more than I wanted to know about the reality of men. I had been conditioned by society to admire men for their intelligence and power, to appreciate them for their superiority and strength. Although I resented this message, at some level I believed it. Entering a man's domain, I expected to discover the marvels of masculinity: wisdom, brilliance, fairness, skill, cleverness, and strength. "It's a man's world," I had been told. And these were the men who controlled it.

What I ultimately discovered was that—not only does every man put his pants on just like any other—he puts them on exactly the same way that a woman would. Given a chance, a woman might even find a way to put them on more efficiently!

I watched my male peers carefully, often in disbelief. I saw how easily some of them cracked under pressure. During our first year of intensive training, one trainee committed suicide because he had failed. Two others had heart attacks; four others turned into fall-down alcoholics who soon lost their jobs and their families as well. These men were out of touch with their true emotions and uncomfortable when confronted with situations that required honest communication. Interactions with other men were usually superficial and selfish, interactions with women were ulterior and insincere. These men were insecure. Without their cars, clothes, looks, and sexual performance, they were deeply alone and empty persons.

I survived in this foreign and hostile male environment for several years. My outrage was frustrated by the reality that corporate change was occurring more slowly than I could tolerate. The price of survival was high. My own personality receded as I took on more and more masculine traits and mastered the skills of masculine thinking. My protective armor hardened every day with each insult and indignity. I began shutting down my emotions, and I soon found myself unable to cry. I could be shrieking hysterically inside, but no tears would appear. I knew that one irrational, oversensitive crying episode would spell professional doom.

Never, I drilled myself, *never* show any sign of weakness. Any hint or suggestion of effeminacy would be professionally detrimental. I hid it all. But somewhere deep within my soul I knew there was an ocean of suppressed anger, hurt, frustration, and humiliation on the verge of breaking and spilling violently into every corner of my life.

I dressed and appeared like a woman, and an attractive one, but I was a "tough chick." It was now 1977, and in a few months I would turn twenty-nine. I drove a string of expensive cars, owned property, traveled internationally. I had bought two airplanes and become a partner in an air charter company. I had also become a workaholic: twelve to fourteen hours a day was my daily regimen. I chain-smoked two packs a day of those chic, skinny, long brown cigarettes. I had achieved elite status. I was so independent and so emotionally insulated that I was beginning to feel isolated from myself. I didn't particularly like myself any-more. There was no more innocence. I had lost my sense of discovery and creativity. Mid-life crisis was coming ten years too early.

I decided to make changes—major ones. I took time off from my career. I became a single mother, an experience that rocked my life and a portion of the Bahá'í community as well. Eventually, I got married. Eventually, I got di-vorced. Eventually, I discovered psychotherapy.

Fortunately, I worked with a psychologist whose remark-able spiritual approach allowed me to recognize the bene-fits as well as the damage done by my individual gender experience. Surviving in the foreign and disapproving cor-porate environment for so many years had not only altered my natural feminine tendencies but had also distorted my reality and created tremendous internal conflict. I had been so long emotionally compensating and sexually counterbal-ancing for professional survival that I was unable to strike a healthy balance between masculine and feminine charac-teristics. Only such a balance, I learned, would allow me to achieve my full potential.

Hours upon hours of prayer, months of discussion, and

years of therapy gradually unlocked the layers of protective defenses and compensated ego. As I made therapeutic progress, I began relating differently to both men and women. I slowly separated assertion from aggression, firmness from defiance, and softness from weakness. Reactions to my newly acquired openness ranged from confusion to delight.

And times had changed. Breaking into the male corporate world had been an unending endurance test. Now, no longer am I *always* the only woman. No longer is the "old boys club" exclusive, even though it is still predominantly male.

I have reflected upon the opportunities, the challenges, the pain, and the rewards. I would not consciously repeat this all again. But, I believe that my unique and remarkable experience was given to me as a means to break through my own personal spiritual blockades and find a healthy, balanced life. It was a gift that helped me to complete a cycle of growth. I will never forget it or regret it.

On Being Black, Female, and Bahá'í in America

by Gloria Haithman

"I REALLY THINK that you have a minority complex, Gloria," my good friend Maggie said to me over a decade ago.

"What's that?" I asked. "Why do you say that?"

"Well, you were born black in a white, racist country, and you were born female in a male-dominated society. The only thing that you had going for you in terms of being in the mainstream of America was that you were born into a Protestant denomination of Christianity. And yet, you chose to become a member of this Bahá'í Faith, which is definitely not a major religion here. Maybe you have a complex about being in the minority. Maybe you don't feel comfortable being in the majority on anything. You really ought to think about that."

This is only a mild example of the countless remarks that very close friends and family have made to me since I declared myself a Bahá'í in 1969. Some expressed the sentiment that I had turned my back on my own people by joining the Bahá'í community, rather than working within the Black Church. My mother, a warm, wonderful woman who always showered me with attention and affection, was deeply disappointed by my change of religion, a feeling she carried with her until she died. After going to several Bahá'í meetings, however, she did concede that Bahá'ís were "nice people socially."

Such feelings, coming from people with whom I have had meaningful relationships, have occasionally made me stop to reevaluate just why I am a Bahá'í. All I have to do is read from any of the Bahá'í Writings, though, and I am immediately reconfirmed. The answer comes through loud and clear. The visions that the Writings inspire in my mind and soul, the feelings they create in my heart, keep me going along on this path. One that I was not born into, but one that I have chosen to pursue.

On the subject of racial equality, the Bahá'í Teachings are unmistakably clear. Shoghi Effendi, in his book *The Advent of Divine Justice* which was addressed to the American Bahá'í Community, repeatedly insists on the importance of eliminating racial prejudice.

Complete freedom from prejudice should be the immediate, the universal and the chief concern of all and sundry members of the Bahá'í community of whatever age, rank, experience, class or color, as all, with no exception, must face its challenging implications, and none can claim, however much he may have progressed along the line to have completely discharged the stern responsibilities that it inculcates.[1]

And again:

As to racial prejudice, the corrosion of which, for well nigh a century, has bitten into the fiber and attacked the whole social structure of American society, it should be regarded as constituting the most vital and challenging issue confronting the Bahá'í community at the present stage of its evolution. The ceaseless exertions which this issue of paramount importance calls for, the sacrifices it must impose, the care and vigilance it demands, the moral courage and fortitude it requires, the tact and sympathy it necessitates, invest this problem, which the American believers are still far from having satisfactorily resolved, with an urgency and importance that cannot be overestimated.[2]

Passages such as these have set a high standard of racial unity and freedom from prejudice for the American Bahá'í community to aspire to. It is necessary, however, to make a distinction between this standard and the actual behavior of the followers of the Faith as it is found in our community life. The Bahá'ís in America, while they may be far ahead of other religions and social organizations in terms of racial unity, are still far from achieving the beautiful ideals extolled in the Bahá'í Scriptures.

'Abdu'l-Bahá admonishes us:

My hope is that the white and the black will be united in perfect love and fellowship, with complete unity and brotherhood. Associate with each other, think of each other, and be like a rose garden. Anyone who goes into a rose garden will see various roses, white, pink, yellow, red, all growing together and replete with adornment.[3]

And again, He says:

Bahá'u'lláh has proclaimed the oneness of the world of humanity. He has caused various nations and divergent creeds to unite. He has declared that difference of race and color is like the variegated beauty of flowers in profusion and beauty—each radiant within itself and although different from the others, lending its own charm to them. Racial differences in the human kingdom is similar. If all the flowers in a garden were of the same color, the effect would be monotonous and wearying to the eye.

Therefore, Bahá'u'lláh hath said that the various races of humankind lend a composite harmony and beauty of color to the whole. Let all associate, therefore, in this great human garden even as flowers grow and blend together side by side without discord or disagreement between them.[4]

With this vision of racial harmony before it, there is an unfortunate tendency in the American Bahá'í community to paint a Pollyannaish picture of itself. Bahá'ís want to believe that they have no prejudice, that they are doing all things well, and are, in fact, approaching perfection. Some Bahá'ís feel that they should not discuss personal struggles or imperfections in the community openly, certainly never at firesides or public meetings.

I recently attended a Bahá'í program in honor of Martin Luther King, Jr. Those present were given an opportunity to talk about the effect that King had on their lives. One Persian Bahá'í spoke and admitted that he had many prejudices against blacks when he arrived in the United States. He explained at length how King had been an inspiration to him and had helped him break the stereotypes that he had previously held about blacks.

Later, he was roundly criticized for speaking so openly in front of non-Bahá'ís. One black Bahá'í was outraged. "How could you feel that way, if you were a Bahá'í?" she asked. The white Bahá'ís were also clearly uncomfortable with his remarks. I heard someone say, "I don't know why we are always stressing integration and race; some things we just have to do among ourselves."

Perhaps because of this desire to paint a positive picture of the Bahá'í community, there have developed a number of apathetic attitudes among Bahá'ís about truly eliminating racial prejudice both inside and outside of our community. I can discuss only a few of these assumptions and positions, which are reflected in comments heard often from Bahá'ís:

Let's not talk about prejudice, let's just talk about unity. How can there be unity in the Bahá'í community if any vestige of racial prejudice is allowed to remain unchallenged? How can we even know what unity means unless we first learn to understand and identify our prejudices? The beloved Guardian, Shoghi Effendi, has characterized racial prejudice as the most vital and challenging issue facing the Bahá'ís of America. How can we not talk about it?

If we don't talk about prejudice within the Bahá'í community, we are in danger of falling into the old social patterns that we find most comfortable. For instance, in one Bahá'í community I lived in there was a youth club that had many dedicated Bahá'í youth involved in it. It was based on Bahá'í principles, and everyone was so happy to see teenagers active and involved in the Faith that no one wanted to point out any problems. There was a lot of talk about unity. But, the club was almost all Persian. It certainly did not reflect racial unity in its membership.

Unity is such a broad and general subject, and it sounds so good, that hardly anyone will disagree with it. But, if we want to apply this concept to specific situations, then we have to talk about prejudice and confront the lack of unity that exists. What use is it for us to talk about the unity of mankind if our Bahá'í groups remain all white, all Persian, or all black.

I don't see color. I don't even think of you as a black person. Unless you hold some negative feelings about my being black, there is nothing wrong with seeing color, mine or anyone else's. Don't ignore my blackness. It has been too big a factor in my life to be overlooked. It is not enough to love me as a person, because you have gotten to know me, while holding different sentiments about others who are like me. I don't want to be divorced from my own people in anyone's mind if that is the price of acceptance.

Well, Bahá'ís love each other, no matter what their color. We don't have any problem with that. We often suppose that we "don't have any problem" when we are at a Bahá'í meeting or event, but then fall back into being just like everyone else when we are away from the Bahá'í community. This is not the standard of Bahá'í life.

Once when my children and I lived briefly in Beverly Hills, we attended a Feast in a lovely large house where we were lavished with hospitality and attention. The host went out of his way to give my daughter a special tour of the house, during which he explained that he was a fifth generation Bahá'í. My daughter was quite impressed with the gentleman and the kindness that he showed her.

A few days later she was in a local store with a couple of her friends after school. She saw this gentleman walking towards them. She was happy to see him and greeted him with a big smile, saying, "Hello!" She spoke to him twice, thinking that he hadn't heard her. He ignored her and kept walking. She felt embarrassed in front of her friends, a fate almost worse than death for a teenager.

She was upset when she told me about it later.

"Maybe he just didn't see you," I said.

"I know he saw me! He looked directly in my eyes and just turned away when I spoke to him," she replied.

Still trying to get the gentleman off the hook for some reason, I suggested that perhaps he just did not recognize her or remember that she had been at the Feast in his house.

"What difference should that have made?" she asked.

I did not have an answer to that, and I still don't.

We should all love each other. Why don't we just act like Bahá'ís? Generally speaking, the assumption here is that we should all be acting like American, middle-class, white, Anglo-Saxon Bahá'ís from a Protestant background. That particular cultural pattern has been accepted as the standard for the Bahá'í community. WASP standards about punctuality, noise levels, space, styles of music, dance, protocol, and manners dominate. There is nothing wrong with that, as long as we do not assign superior moral value to these customs and habits and identify them with the Bahá'í Faith.

There is also the need to keep in mind that the goal of our community is unity in diversity, not unity through uniformity. Various cultures and styles should be reflected in the activities of the Bahá'í community. That is the only way that the beautiful human flower garden, alluded to so often by 'Abdu'l-Bahá in His talks and Writings, will reach the full bloom of its potential.

At a typical Bahá'í Feast, for example, the normal mode of communication is for one person to talk while everyone else listens. There is usually an absence of music, and almost never any group singing. The emphasis is on the presentation of information, rather than on sharing or emotional release. Everyone is expected to remain calm and businesslike. Any deviation from the established program is likely to make people uncomfortable.

Such an atmosphere is, however, foreign to black culture. It is not a "Bahá'í" way of doing things, but rather a European model adapted to the Bahá'í community. In a black church, for instance, if a minister spoke to the congregation and everyone just sat there like they do in the Bahá'í community, he would be devastated. Those listening are expected to call out words of encouragement, nod and hum, connect with their eyes, and communicate their feelings spontaneously. The program is always flexible, and there is a lot of improvisation and sharing and freedom of movement. Our Bahá'í community life would be much richer if we could incorporate some aspects of black culture.

I attended a Bahá'í meeting once where both blacks and whites were present in fairly large numbers. Some of us stayed after the meeting to clean up, and at one point there were only black Bahá'ís left. Unconsciously we all started talking louder, with three or four conversations going at once, and all of us going in and out of the conversations with everyone else. The mood was more animated and there was more laughter. Suddenly, it dawned on us what had happened. I was amazed at how, immediately after the last white Bahá'í left, without anybody saying anything, our mode of conversation had changed. Somehow this way of talking to each other had not seemed acceptable before. One of the black Bahá'ís laughed and said, "Uh-oh, this is why they don't want us in the neighborhood."

Bahá'ís all believe in integration, and blacks are fully integrated into Bahá'í life. The major problem with integration in our society is that it has been a one-way street. The American mainstream that everyone is trying to integrate into is, in reality, the American whitestream. Again, the danger is that diversity of culture will be ignored or lost.

In the Bahá'í community, integration should be different. It should be a multifaceted process, with many roads and avenues going in both directions. It should be a process characterized by mutual respect and reciprocity. We should be willing to allow many cultures to influence us, not simply to admit blacks and other minorities into a Bahá'í community that goes along with business as usual.

The Black Woman's Experience. One of the things I feel could be helpful to the Bahá'í community is a greater awareness and understanding of the unique history, perspective, culture, and feeling of black American women. These women have faced challenges and problems that no other women in this country have faced. A well-known poem by a black poet expresses in its lament some of the strength and determination of black women:

> Well, son, I'll tell you:
> Life for me ain't been no crystal stair.
> It's had tacks in it,
> And splinters,
> And boards torn up,
> And places with no carpets on the floor—
> Bare.
> But all the time
> I'se been a-climbin' on
> And reachin' landin's
> And turnin' corners,
> And sometimes goin' in the dark
> Where there ain't been no light,
> So boy, don't you turn back,
> Don't you set down on the steps
> Cause you finds it kiner hard.
> Don't you fall now—
> For I'se still goin', honey,
> I'se still climbin'
> And life for me ain't been no crystal stair.[5]

As one who was born into that culture, I would like to share some of my own perspectives about being black and female in America. First, black women here bear the double burden of being victims of both racism and sexism. Contrary to what most people seem to think, these are not the same kinds of things. Certainly racism and sexism share similar characteristics: Both the racist and the sexist relegate others to an inferior status and position; they both have a pathological need to see themselves as superior to others, somehow special or chosen; and they both have created social structures designed to keep others in the places where they have decided they belong. The same person may often be a racist and a sexist, but this is not always the case.

Racism and sexism are closely related evils that weigh heavily on the very souls of black sisters, but racism is considered by most of them to be the most dangerous and insidious, because it develops more intense, hardened, unreasonable, and uncompromising aversion, fear, hatred, and violence. I don't think that anyone has ever been lynched as a result of sexism. All men have some positive relations with women—every sexist had a mother, and probably has a wife, a lover, or a daughter. This provides women, no matter how oppressed they are, with a means to influence and affect their sexist men. The racist, on the other hand, need have no relationship at all with black people, except as an object of undiluted hatred.

Therefore, although concerned about both, most black American women are far more concerned about racism. This gives them a different set of priorities than those of white women. Besides having a history of racism within its own ranks, the Women's Movement in America has never made any attempt to distinguish between the interests and concerns of black and white women. The problems and priorities of whites have been either automatically assumed to be the problems and concerns of everyone else, or they are considered to be more important than the problems and concerns of non-whites.

Black women are not offended when their men call them *baby*. They are usually pleased and flattered, and glad that they were not called *bitch* instead. Black women are not annoyed if a man opens a door for them. They are glad that it was not slammed in their face. Black women are not interested in developing ways to make themselves more independent of black men. They are already independent. On the contrary, they are concerned with how they can establish better and more permanent relations with the opposite sex.

On other issues, one can see even more of a divergence between the perspectives of black women and those of whites. For example, the question of whether to work outside the home or stay home to raise children, which is so central to the women's movement, is utterly irrelevant to most black women in America. Most of us have always worked outside the home. The issue for us is not whether or not to work, but what kind of work can be found. In the past, our employment has often been limited to menial, servile, low-ranking jobs.

It is frustrating for blacks to read in the literature of the women's movement, and in other sources, that American women entered the work force in significant numbers during World War II, and that they have remained there ever since. This is true of white women, but does not address the work experience of black American women. Assumptions like this make it seem as if black women do not exist, even though blacks make up more than one-tenth of the American population. Black women were brought to this country to work as slaves. The first of us arrived before the Mayflower, and we have always been working.

Likewise, in the areas of economic power, family relations, self-concept, and basic identity, black women have had a fundamentally different experience in America than have whites. The story of black women has been a continuous saga of struggle: struggle through slavery, struggle for survival, struggle for self-esteem and positive self-image.

Black women have been assaulted by stereotypes and analyzed by social scientists since they first set foot in America. Because of the roles they have had to play, black women have developed unique strategies, styles, outlooks, perspectives, and priorities. Because of this, they have often been portrayed negatively or compared unfavorably to white women, without regard for their unique strengths and skills.

White women, in general, from the time of slavery and up to recent decades, were valued for being dependent and decorative. Their concerns and activities were usually limited and revolved around their homes and children. White physical features were accepted as the standard of beauty for all women.

Black women, on the other hand, have been valued within their community for their ability to work hard, to take care of themselves and their families, and to survive and persevere against all odds. Their role models are mothers and grandmothers who were strong and self-reliant. Black women have always operated in circles outside of their homes, as well as within the family. They have always assumed part of the responsibility for the economic support of their children, and often for the other members of their families. And because of these experiences they have developed unique strategies, styles, outlooks, perspectives, and priorities.

Within the black community, education and political power have always been recognized as means to greater opportunity for black people. And black women have been at the forefront of acquiring both. They often received a better education than black men, because it was decided within black families that, if a choice had to be made, the daughter should be educated before the son. This was done to protect the daughter. Since it was assumed that she would have to work outside of the home even after marriage, without an education her jobs would be limited to hard labor in the field, or domestic work in white kitchens where she would be vulnerable to the attacks of white men. Many families felt that their sons, being male, could better handle the hard jobs that involved heavy labor and would have a wider range of menial jobs available to them, such as construction or railroad work. Girls were also felt to be more likely to use their resources to take care of their children when they grew up, and to take care of their own parents in sickness or old age.

Since the forces of racism and segregation, through most of American history, served to keep the black family impoverished—in a state of bare economic survival, black women have always had to assume a part of the responsibility of supporting their families. This is not to say that black men did not also struggle to provide adequately for their families. But because of the restrictions on their employment and their generally low wages, they could not act as the sole breadwinners. The black community, including its women, learned to develop inner resources—spiritual, mental, social, and artistic—that provided the strength needed to survive in a hostile environment. As a result, in many ways, the black woman is more liberated than her white counterpart. She has less need to be concerned about what men think about anything. She is much more independent of men, both economically and psychologically.

I can remember working a few years ago with a group that sold encyclopaedias. We were planning a special promotion that would involve working evenings. One of the others, a lively, gray-haired, white woman—one of our most active salespersons—sadly explained that she would not be able to participate in this project because her husband would not "let her."

At first I thought that she must be joking, or that she just didn't want to do it and was using her husband as an excuse. She went on to say how he would never "let her" do anything that took her away from home after 6 P.M. She could not even go with a group of friends to a movie or religious celebration, unless it was with her husband. It did not seem to be so much a concern for her safety as the need to be controlling. He could, and often did, go places without her after 6 P.M. when he wanted to, but she did not have the same privilege.

I remember finding it almost impossible to comprehend how any mature adult could allow someone else, male or female, to set such limits for them. I became conscious after that of women making statements about what their husbands or boyfriends would or would not "let them do." In almost every case, the woman who speaks in those terms is white.

Black women are proud of being women. They have a real sense of sisterhood and a strong network of support. Normally, they see themselves as fully equal to men, and they have trouble understanding the hostility and resentment that many white women feel toward men because of unequal treatment.

When I went to college, besides getting a degree, everyone in my family expected me to join a black sorority. The sororities provided an important network for black women. None of us thought of joining a men's organization—like the Rotary Club, for example—because there was no advantage to being in a black men's group that could not be found in a sorority. The women's groups were independent, more active, and stronger than the men's groups.

The real concern of black women was to establish better relations with black men. We assumed that we already had equal rights. But there are one-third more adult black women than adult black men, and relations between the sexes are often problematic. Partially, this is due to economic factors, like high unemployment among men. But it is also caused by a sort of black female chauvinism that regards men as very desirable, but definitely dispensable. As Diana Ross sang in one line of her hit tune "One Monkey Don't Stop No Show": "I love you, but I can live without you!"

The independence of black women has caused problems for relationships. Black men often complain that black women "don't know how to treat a man." This usually means that black women are seldom willing to put up with mistreatment. If a relationship isn't working, they are willing to say, "Okay, bye. I'm getting on with my life." But it also reflects an unwillingness on their part to play the traditional dependent, accommodating female roles.

At my job, I was involved with two other women in a deep and serious discussion one day. Suddenly, the director of the program rushed into the office. He was tired and sweaty, and he obviously had not taken a shower after jogging to work. He went into his office and one of the women spoke to him. "Oh, you look so tired. Did you run today?" she said, in a high, sweet, little-girl voice. And she seemed so concerned about him, so accommodating. I turned around because I thought that another woman had entered the room. Her voice had changed so much that I thought she was someone else. I was shocked.

I had said nothing, but my unspoken reaction had been: How dare you come into this office all sweaty like that! What is your problem? Then I thought to myself: Well, no wonder they like them better! We aren't willing to put up with nearly as much. And we don't use little-girl voices unless we're in love.

Black Women in the American Bahá'í Community. The American community has attracted more black women than black men. There are no doubt many reasons for this, among which is the simple one that there are significantly more black women than black men in America. According to the 1980 census, for all age groups, there were 89.1 black males for every 100 black females, and the gap widens as the age level increases.

However, these statistics alone do not fully explain the high disproportion of black men to black women among Bahá'ís. An official scientific study may be needed to obtain an accurate assessment of this phenomenon. However, I would like to share some of what is merely my own speculation about the current situation.

Part of the reason, I feel, is hinged in history. When the American Bahá'í community began to expand beyond a small circle of wealthy, socially sophisticated whites, it attracted many black people because of its sponsorship of and participation in the Race Amity Conferences. Often important organizations in the black community were invited to participate, and thus some of their members were exposed to the Bahá'í Teachings for the first time. Women were, and still are, prominent in those organizations, as well as in the black American community as a whole. Several of them became Bahá'ís and also brought in some of their friends. Unfortunately, the American Bahá'í community no longer pursues the same effective kind of outreach to the black community that it once did.

I also think that the American Bahá'í community tends to attract men (both black and white) who are successful in at least fording, if not splashing about in, that good old mainstream of American society. Others may not feel totally comfortable in the community as it exists today. I have a Bahá'í friend who says he still believes in Bahá'u'lláh and obeys His laws, but who has chosen to not be active in the community on any level. He feels that the American Bahá'í community is not able to deal with black men who are "outspoken," or who do not conform to certain white standards. He perceives the community as being dominated by what he has described as "the same people who control everything else in the world, who make all the major decisions, and who run, and often ruin, everyone's life: middle-aged white men." He also feels that the American Bahá'í community is not "actively concerned" about black people, even though it "does a lot of talking" about unity and racial harmony. He feels that he can never have "a real voice" in the community. And so, he has decided that his limited efforts and energy are best spent working directly on the challenges presented to black Americans, rather than indirectly through the Bahá'í activities which, he believes, have no significant impact in the black community at this time. I do not agree with most of his views or I would have done as he did. But his challenge is a serious one.

At any rate, black American women are actively involved in and deeply committed to the American Bahá'í community. They have made many important contributions in a variety of ways. They find, however, that there are few men within the community whom they can marry and raise families with. For black women, the problem of the small

number of black men in the community is complicated by
another fact that, just as in the non-Bahá'í community,
black men are far more likely to marry outside of their race
than are black women.

Intermarriage, as Bahá'ís know, is fully accepted and
even encouraged in the Bahá'í Teachings and by the community. However, this aspect of the Teachings has been
taken far more seriously by the relatively few black men in
the American Bahá'í community than by the Bahá'í men of
other races. One has only to make a quick survey, from the
highest levels of leadership in the American Bahá'í community to the grass roots, to confirm this trend. When men of
other races do marry across racial lines, it is rarely to a
black woman. I have heard comments and complaints
about this tendency countless times over the years from
other black Bahá'í women, yet I have never heard it discussed seriously and openly with members of the Bahá'í
community who are not black.

The reasons for this trend are numerous and speculative.
The sources may include the negative stereotypes of black
women which are projected so successfully in the general,
non-Bahá'í community. It is most frustrating to recognize
that the same attitudes are alive and well within the Bahá'í
community. In my opinion, this is one area in which the Bahá'í community is not that far ahead of others, even though
the Teachings clearly are.

The advice that I give to young black women, like my
own daughter, is to look outside the American Bahá'í community for a mate. I am sure that there are those who will
disagree with me on that point, but I sincerely believe that
at this stage of development in our American community,
this is the best policy for a black American woman to follow. I realize that this is not an ideal solution. If one's husband is not a Bahá'í and is committed to another religion
this may be a source of some conflict. Also, if a boyfriend is
not a Bahá'í, it may be more difficult to adhere to Bahá'í

standards in the relationship. However, the alternative for most black women is to stand by and watch the great rush toward women of all other races by the men in the Bahá'í community including those of their own race and to look forward to a life of unwanted celibacy.

Someone suggested to my daughter that if she really wanted a Bahá'í husband, she should move to another country—to Europe, or Africa, or Asia, or almost anywhere else—because she would certainly "be a hit" in the Bahá'í communities there. I rather resented that kind of advice because it seemed that, as in so many other things, the black woman was expected to make an extra effort just to enjoy such basic things as marriage and family.

But, on the other hand, extraordinary efforts have always been required of black women. The problem of finding a mate within the Bahá'í community is not, after all, the most pressing one for all black women in America. The most important issue for black women, in my opinion, is not to forget the lessons learned from our noble foremothers whose strength and fortitude nurtured a race through harrowing hard times and spawned a race of people who elicit both castigation and fascination from others. Their children have made an indelible imprint upon the fabric of humanity. Ours is the task of continuing the struggle to eliminate all forms and traces of the racism that has victimized our people, and so many others.

This mission is described so sweetly and succinctly in a poem by Maya Angelou:

> You may write me down in history
> With your bitter, twisted lies.
> You may trod me in the very dust,
> But still, like dust, I'll rise.
>
> You may shoot me with your words,
> You may cut me with your eyes,

You may kill me with your hatefulness,
But still, like air, I'll rise.

Out of the sheets of history's shame,
I rise.
Up from a past that's rooted in pain,
I rise.
I'm a black ocean, leaping and wide,
Welling and swelling I bear in the tide.

Leaving behind nights of terror and fear,
I rise.
Into a daybreak that's wondrously clear,
I rise.
Bringing the gifts that my ancestors gave,
I am the dream and the hope of the slave.
I rise
I rise
I rise.[6]

The Bahá'í Teachings flow like healing waters from the Fount of Wisdom to eradicate the pains of the past and to lead us to the pleasures of true unity as envisioned in the principle of the oneness of mankind. As Hand of the Cause, Louis Gregory, said over 60 years ago at the Eighteenth Annual Convention of the Bahá'ís of the United States and Canada in 1926:

Who-ever stands upon the exalted principle [the unity of humanity] will never be shaken by the shifting sands of time; who-ever stands upon this exalted principle, like the lever of Archimedes, will move the world.[7]

Our task as black women is to challenge our beloved Bahá'í communities to achieve a higher level of integration than that achieved by the general non-Bahá'í community.

We do not aspire to be like whites, as some people seem to want to. We do not aspire to be like men, as some women seem to want to. We bring and offer our special assets to the table of unity.

The task of tending to the flower garden of humanity and promoting that association which enables all to "grow and blend together" is ours. As we pursue these often thankless tasks and continue to strive in the manner that is unique to being black and female in America, we can take solace and find inspiration in the following words of 'Abdu'l-Bahá which were written to a woman of color:

> *O thou who art pure in heart, sanctified in spirit, peerless in character, beauteous in face! Thy photograph hath been received revealing thy physical frame in the utmost grace and the best appearance. Thou art dark in countenance and bright in character. Thou art like unto the pupil of the eye which is dark in colour, yet it is the fount of light and the revealer of the contingent world.*
>
> *I have not forgotten nor will I forget thee. I beseech God that He may graciously make thee the sign of His bounty amidst mankind, illumine thy face with the light of such blessings as are vouchsafed by the merciful Lord, single thee out of His love in this age which is distinguished among all the past ages and centuries.*[8]

Notes

1. Shoghi Effendi, *The Advent of Divine Justice* (Wilmette, Ill., Bahá'í Publishing Trust, 1939) p. 32.

2. Ibid., p. 33–34.

3. 'Abdu'l-Bahá, *The Promulgation of Universal Peace*, comp. by Howard MacNutt, 2nd ed. (Wilmette, Ill., Bahá'í Publishing Trust, 1982) pp. 427–28.

4. Ibid., pp. 68–69.

5. Langston Hughes, in *Caroling Dusk: An Anthology of Verse by Negro Poets*, ed. by Countee Cullen (New York: Harper and Bros., Publishers, 1927) pp. 151–52.

6. Maya Angelou, *Still I Rise* (New York: Random House, 1978) pp. 41–42.

7. Quoted in Gayle Morrison, *To Move the World* (Wilmette, Ill.: Bahá'í Publishing Trust, 1982) p. 321.

8. 'Abdu'l-Bahá, *Selections from the Writings of 'Abdu'l-Bahá*, trans. by a Committee at the Bahá'í World Center and Marzieh Gail (Haifa: Bahá'í World Centre, 1978) p. 114.

Becoming a Man

by Sidney Morrison

BY AGE EIGHT, I still played with dolls and told stories about princes and princesses in fantastic kingdoms where anything was possible. My father came into my room one day and found paper dolls and their clothes scattered on the table. He decided to spank me. I pleaded with him, but he would not listen. He pulled me between his legs—a vise which made it almost impossible to move—and I yelled, waiting for the fall of his thick, right hand. He never used a belt.

Suddenly his legs slackened; he pulled me up and pushed me into the hall toward the living room, calling for the rest of the family to meet there. When my mother, my two brothers, and my sister arrived, he quickly left and returned with my sister's powder blue crinoline dress. Throwing it at me, he said, "Put it on!"

Stunned, I only gaped at him.

"Put it on now!" he demanded.

"Please don't make me, daddy," I said, looking to my mother for help.

She stood at the door behind everyone else, and whispered, "Sissy."

191

I started to cry.

My tears seemed to make my father angrier. "Now!" he repeated as his fists tightened.

Fearing his fist, I stepped into the dress; my hands shook as I pulled it over my shoes and pants. I closed my eyes. My brothers laughed. Unable to bear the distance which separated me from my family, I promised to play basketball, my father's favorite sport. Smiling, he sent me from the room after lecturing me about "real boys."

But simply being on the court was not enough; I had to play well too. Unfortunately, I could not run fast enough, jump high enough, or pass the ball quickly enough. Every mistake seemed to earn a jeer, and I became more and more incompetent.

I liked books instead—histories, biographies, novels, plays. I read under the sheets with a flashlight. I read on the streets, sitting on the curb or on the apartment house stoop, and earned the title "the professor" from the neighborhood kids. The library, where I would spend hours, became my favorite place. There I enjoyed the silent freedom to explore the world beyond my Bronx, New York street; there I gathered information with which I could impress my critics. One book, a beautifully illustrated history of costumes, from the Egyptians to the present—a pageant of armored knights, powdered-wigged gentlemen in white tights and heels, dandies with top hats and cravats, and ladies with bustles, hooped skirts, or chastity belts—so impressed me that I stole it when I was eleven. I still have the book, a reminder that it was easier for me to steal than to play basketball.

Because I was afraid to go out, my mother knew how to punish me. All she had to say was: "Go outside and play." I knew what would happen. Teams would be formed and I would be the last to be selected, reluctantly chosen to keep the numbers even. Sometimes the team captain would sneer as he gestured me over to his side, convinced that my presence made defeat inevitable. If I was an extra, few volunteered to recruit another so that I could play. The popularity of my brothers, however, usually ensured a place for me. Few wanted to cross my younger brother Mike, who could slice a head off with his sharp tongue. But even he could not prevent my tactical mistakes and the verbal abuse which they invited. In fact, he often led the chorus:

"Sissy!"

"Fag!"

"He/She!"

Despite this, I wanted to be accepted by the boys on the block; through them I was defining myself, my masculinity. When we traveled in packs through the street, roller skating in a single row and demonstrating our agility as we passed over huge manholes, or when we played war, assaulting battlements of snow and capturing trashcan targets, I felt the power of the bond between us, a bond created by a mutual need to conquer, impress, produce, or win.

I yearned for that single, awesome act that would ensure my everlasting membership in the charmed circle of the "real boys." But I learned that one failure, one mistake, one weakness could justify banishment; and I would have to start over to prove myself worthy once more. As Norman Mailer once observed: "Nobody was born a man; you earned your manhood, provided you were good enough, bold enough."

I was not bold enough. My experiment with the Boy Scouts was a disaster. I was not impressed with the badges or the uniforms, and I could not figure out what the Bible and the American flag had to do with each other. My troop's trip to the forests of Staten Island in the middle of winter convinced me that I lacked the necessary fortitude.

We were supposed to stay in a heated cabin, sleep on bunkbeds, and cook our meals on electric stoves. For some obscure reason, our leader did not have the key to the cabin when we arrived. And so, we were forced to spend the weekend in lean-tos, three-sided wood structures that provided inadequate protection from the cold rain that soaked the blanket serving as a fourth wall. We slept on the hard floor, cooked outside. I struggled to hold a skillet over the fire, so numb were my hands. My gloves were useless, as were my boots. I secretly envied the boy who went home early with frostbite.

I quit the Boy Scouts after a week, breaking another rule: Real boys don't quit. Our culture teaches that when the going gets tough, the tough get going. Winners don't quit; quitters don't win. And, of course, they fight to the death.

I started a fight I did not want to get into, but according to the code, a slur against one's mother could not be accepted with impunity. That the offending boy was older and bigger did not matter; I had to fight. The word was out: Sidney—how I hated the name—was going to fight Cleophus behind the apartment building. A large crowd gathered to watch Cleophus kick my butt.

At first I enjoyed everyone's surprise; I had actually shown up. I had forgotten that my opponent was notorious for his restless, almost manic energy. He never tired, punching me until he had to be pulled off. And he didn't care where he hit me. (Somehow I thought he would leave my face alone.) My pride hurt more than my lips. I felt naked and isolated, surrounded by a crowd which demanded more pain, more blood, as it laughed at my defeat. That was my first fight, and my last.

I was also supposed to like competitive sport. One play in a single football game, however, made me a skeptic. As usual, I was a reluctant last choice, and I played poorly. But during one down I somehow caught the pass and ran with it. The thrill of this achievement overwhelmed me. I was exhilarated by my speed. I seemed to fly, throwing my head back as I saw the trees in the park pass by, eluding the line determined to catch me. Or so I thought. When I passed the goal line, I jumped up and down, joyous at my first touchdown. Calmer, I soon realized that no one had followed to share my triumph. Appalled by such callousness, I strode over to both teams. They informed me through contemptuous laughter that I had run the wrong way.

My entire flesh seemed to burn. I wanted to burrow into the ground, hide somehow. I put the football on the ground and walked away from the game—and from competitive sports. Almost thirty years later, I still don't play. And I don't watch.

I wanted to be told that I was all right. Only the girls seemed to accept me. They certainly were not anxious about their identities; no one questioned their femininity, granted it one day and withdrew it the next. I enjoyed their company and played their games. I became effeminate, adapting to my peers.

But I never wanted to become a girl, and when I reached adolescence, I wanted to do what every boy said that they had already done.

There it was in my high school annual: a photograph which confirmed in black and white my negative self-image. I stared at the mole on my too-high forehead, the gap between my two front teeth, my thick lips, my wide nostrils, my neck hidden by a severely buttoned collar— and, worst of all, my glasses which sat tilted on my nose like a propeller poised for flight. Why hadn't the photographer suggested a retake? I wondered, enraged by his insensitivity. I tore the offending page from my annual, but that only gave me momentary relief from the intense embarrassment I felt. In every other yearbook lay the proof that I was a nerd, a wimp, a geek, a jerk.

Yet I remained hopeful. One trip to the boy's locker room had confirmed that I was not gifted with the measurements that I heard every girl craved. But I was sure that Jill, who sat next to me in my English class, would one day realize my true qualifications for that carnal embrace I dreamed about daily. She was beautiful, intelligent, and sophisticated. I admired her maturity. I also appreciated her respect for my scholastic ability; she asked for my help with difficult assignments and acknowledged my insights. We were friends.

My infatuation turned instantly to hatred when she came to the senior prom with a college man, six feet three or four and strikingly handsome. Of course, I hadn't had the nerve to ask her to go to the prom with me. I had settled on Janice, ugly but nice—who I heard liked me for some reason or other.

The evening began with high hopes. When I put on my tuxedo with its white jacket and black cummerbund, my mother complimented my physical appearance for the first time I could remember: "Sidney, I didn't realize that you could be so handsome." Looking into the mirror, I too was surprised. But this new vision also dazzled me. Jill would be swept away. She would abandon her date and dance with me dance after dance.

Unfortunately, I almost missed the prom. The boy who had the car got lost and never called to ask for directions. After two hours of waiting, Janice, whom I called repeatedly to assure her that everything would work out, went to bed in despair. My parents did not have a car, so I could not ask them to take us. I finally asked a neighbor who drove me to Janice's house, where her mother received me with stupefied surprise. In my excitement, I had neglected to call to tell her I was coming. Janice dressed quickly; she had a gorgeous pink brocade dress which fell to the floor. But her wig was too apparently that, a piece with obvious open gaps.

With so incredible a delay, I expected us to be absolutely the last arrivals. But Jill and her date arrived after we did. Their tardiness seemed a contemptuous dismissal of the importance of the evening, an adult sneer at our juvenile revels. As we danced, I tried to ignore them. But my resolve failed me and I stared compulsively, struggling to meet the standard they set. She was an ice princess, impossible to reach; he a shining knight, inspiring fear.

I felt betrayed. I was convinced that girls preferred the guys who kicked sand into the faces of us skinny ones. In college I witnessed further proof of this preference. All the beautiful girls seemed to land on the arms of the jocks with twenty-one inch necks. Fearing another rejection, I avoided romantic relationships and focused instead on my studies— another area in which I had to prove I was good enough. I went to class and studied for hours in the stacks of the library, where couples met to grope and also study. And yet I was not satisfied; my sense of responsibility did not compensate for the aching emptiness. I was alone. My grades were mediocre,except in history, my first love. I wondered, Is this all? I expected duty to bestow greater pleasure; it did nothing but justify habit. I swam in self-pity. When that started to bore even me, I really began to worry.

Then I discovered the Bahá'í Faith.

At first, I did not realize what effect this would have on my masculinity. I was attracted to the message of unity and found its ideas reasonable and exciting. Gradually, I found something else, a definition of self which transcended cultural expectations. I was told that I was worthy, that I was good enough—not because I had accomplished something of value, but because I existed, a creation of God.

"O Son of Man!" writes Bahá'u'lláh, the Prophet and Founder of the Bahá'í Faith, *"Thou art My dominion and My dominion perisheth not, wherefore fearest thou thy perishing? Thou art My light and My light shall never be extinguished, why dost thou dread extinction? Thou art My glory and My glory fadeth not."*

I did not realize the impact these words had on me until I was drafted into U.S. Army, which seemed to have rounded up every neighborhood bully in the nation to give them drill sergeant's stripes. Our drill instructors knew where we new recruits were most vulnerable—between our legs. And they never tired of reminding us of what we did not have. The ultimate insult was to characterize us as "pussies."

Our leaders claimed that they had a noble mission, to mold us into "real men," and that the only way to achieve this end was to exhaust us mentally and physically and then rebuild. We were assured that the training, which consisted of predawn runs, thousands of pushups, surprise inspections of polished shoes and buckles, endless hours of kitchen patrol, and little sleep, would grant us the essential equipment. Manhood was the only issue.

I protested only once.

During that first week I filled out countless forms, including one for my dog tags on which I had to declare my name, serial number, blood type, and religious preference. Although I did not see "Bahá'í" listed on the wall, I wrote the word down anyway. When I received my metal plates after waiting for about an hour, I stared at the two tags incredulously. Replacing "Bahá'í" was the meaningless word "Other." Suddenly I saw myself dead in Vietnam, my coffin wrapped in a huge flag, my body buried with military rites against my wishes. If I'm going to die, I thought, I'll be damned if the Army will have the final word on who I am and what I die for. Furious, I marched up to the little window, shaking the tags in my fist.

"What in the hell is this?" I shouted, forgetting that such insubordination could mean eternal pushups, the dreaded Article 15, or the stockade.

The corporal's answer was incredibly stupid. "We don't have that word," he said with all the smugness of minor officialdom.

I looked around his overweight body to the machine which printed the tags; it was obvious that letters, not words, were being inscribed. "You have a *B*, don't you?" I screamed. "You have an *H*, and an *A*, and an *I*. The word is spelled B-A-H-A-I, and I'm not leaving until you put it on these tags."

Looking at me like I was a wild man, he immediately jumped off his stool and had the machinist inscribe the word. Keeping his distance, he handed the tags to me as if I were going to bite. I checked for the required word and suddenly I began to tremble, realizing now that I could be punished severely for daring to challenge even one small part of the system. I returned to the formation meeker than before.

No one said a word, but I could see fear, confusion, and hostility in scores of eyes. Some eyes accused me of endangering the group; even a minor infraction, a mere slip in the tuck of a sheet, could mean hours of peeling potatoes or cleaning toilets for everybody.

The sergeant smirked; then he ordered us all to attention and, without further comment, sent us to our next assignment.

I took no pride in my protest. I was just relieved that no one said anything about it. After only a week in the Army I knew that putting myself before the security of the platoon, the ultimate betrayal, would be forgiven only once. A year later I went to Vietnam, a conscientious objector without weapons training, a combat medic without a gun. I didn't think too much about this. I was too worried about stepping on a land mine and blowing up. Besides, the guys in my platoon protected me, determined to keep me safe to help them when they tripped a mine or received a bullet in the back.

I was also worried that they would find out that I was a virgin, a status inconceivable for a black guy from California, the land of the love-in and marijuana in every backyard. When they shared their sexual exploits, I listened but said little. The language revealed an incredible ignorance of human sexuality. So there I was, the inexperienced medic, teaching young men the correct vocabulary for sexual technique and for nether parts of the human anatomy. Some of the words amused them, and they chanted the more exotic ones as if these had the power to conjure up the acts themselves.

My buddies did not need magic, however. Sex was readily available. Mothers peddled their daughters, brothers sold their sisters, girls offered themselves, trading a little "boom boom" for a little money. On several occasions, a single industrious woman would take on the entire platoon. The men simply lined up, waiting their turn in a single file. Invariably the experience inside the bunker required a detailed commentary outside of it. Everyone spoke about the good "piece" and bragged that their unique performance had "really turned her on." I wondered how she felt about all this, but I did not say anything. Nobody ever talked about her.

My Bahá'í values and the fear of an incurable venereal disease kept me from standing in line, but the pressure was intense. Our solidarity was being affirmed by this ritualized fornication and strutting bravado; real men and true brothers sport together. These impulses, revealing connections between violence, misogyny, and that recurring demand for men to prove themselves, can have grotesque and tragic consequences: Several veterans have told about their participation in "gang bangs" that were followed by murder.

Fortunately, I did not see a gang rape in Vietnam. But I sensed the potential for violence, a jungle within us more dangerous perhaps than the jungle around us. And so I held fast to my religious principles, aware that fear, exhaustion, and the need to belong could provoke the betrayal of them at any moment.

I didn't know if anyone knew or cared about my religious commitment until near the end of my tour of duty. Having earned a "rear" job after seven months of duty as an infantry platoon medic, I filled my nights, as many "rears" did, with trips to the club. There we enjoyed anyone who ventured to come and entertain us. One night, as I waited for the show to begin, I heard a photographer behind me boast about how he was going out into the field with only a single pistol; obnoxious, he went on and on about it. Finally, Sergeant Shields, a young man I admired but did not know well, lost his patience and said, "That's nothing. Now, Doc Morrison here didn't carry anything, no rifle, no pistol, nothing. Now, he has balls!"

I did not see my conscientious objection as an act of courage, just another component of my belief system. And yet Sergeant Shields' compliment moved me deeply. At that moment I attained that recognition which I had hungered for as a boy; and what pleased me was the fact that I received it without any compromise of my integrity. My religious identity naturally reinforced my manhood.

Two months before, I was awarded a bronze star with a "V" for valor under fire after I ran through a mine field to help the injured. A general had flown out in a helicopter to pin this medal on me as I stood in formation in a fire support base twenty-five miles north of Saigon. But that moment with Shields in the club was a prouder moment. In fact, it was one of the best of my life.

When does one become a man?

Returning from Vietnam, I felt more like one. "Every man needs a war," said Hemingway. I disagree, but I needed mine. I had survived and endured; the impossible became true. Sidney Morrison could sleep in the muck of rice paddies, calmly remove leeches from his legs, eat out of cans, walk for miles in humid jungle without fainting, bandage torn flesh without flinching. And somehow the terror of starry nights, when waiting to be killed allowed only four hours' uneasy sleep, had not destroyed my hopes for the future. I was ready to continue with my life, finish my education, get a job, find a wife, raise a family. Having found a measure of inner strength, I was now able to accept some of the trappings of masculinity.

I changed the way I looked. I put on some muscles. I allowed my hair to grow and bought clothes from fashionable stores; my glasses were imports from Italy. Then I fell in love with an old friend who accepted my vulnerability. She was the first to know how I felt when my father made me wear that blue dress. I cried with her, recalling the devastating recognition that the powerful, distant man whom I loved and admired wanted to hurt me. With her I was comfortable being myself.

We married.

I soon discovered that I, despite my respect for my wife, carried into our marriage some of the cultural baggage which diminishes women. She made this clear one perfect Sunday afternoon.

I sat on the living room sofa reading the Sunday paper and listening to a Mozart piano concerto. My wife was cleaning the house and preparing dinner; her family was coming that evening. Suddenly, I heard the slamming of cupboards and the loud clatter of pots. The noise became louder and louder. Then Karan appeared at the kitchen door, her blue eyes wide and accusing: "So you think that you're too good for the work that has to be done, don't you?" she asked scornfully.

"What?" I replied, surprised by her tone and by the question. I ironed my own clothes, and I cooked on occasion.

"I work too, you know. What makes you think that you are entitled to sit around when I have to clean the house, cook the food, and do the laundry besides?"

I glanced at the cart of dirty clothes waiting to be taken to the laundromat. Karan had left it at the front door so that when some free time became available she could leave quickly. She had run out of time. I jumped up from the sofa and took the laundry to be washed without saying a word, for I knew immediately that she was right. I believed that I had a man's prerogative to which she had no claim.

Where did such an idea come from? I asked myself. If some one had asked me if I held such an assumption I would have scoffed; after all, I believed in the equality of men and women. Or did I really believe in it. I had to reconsider.

The process is difficult. Our culture demands that I be a cross between John Wayne, the Chase Manhattan Bank, and Hugh Hefner and extols this prototype in magazines and books, on records and on television. The pressure is difficult to resist: As a high school history teacher, I was ashamed to tell my oldest son my annual salary because masculinity is rated by the number of digits on the monthly check. Sometimes I am uncomfortable when my wife, who is mechanically gifted, repairs a leaking faucet and my youngest son wonders aloud: "Isn't a man supposed to do this?" Occasionally, I envy the movie star whose very eyes drive women to indiscretion. And I am still surprised to find that when I have a conflict with my children—two sons and a daughter—I become my own father: stern, distant, intransigent, and loud. The models from childhood stay with us.

And yet, I can be so touched by a performance of Mozart that I will cry. I care about the clothes I wear. I appreciate the aesthetics of good interior design. I iron, and change the baby's diaper. These traditionally female actions are viewed with suspicion. And there is a fear that feminine values and emotions, if allowed free expression, will make men incompetent in an unjust, competitive world. It's a jungle out there, claims the old adage, and you have to be hard and strong to survive. After years of education and reflection, I see the nonsense in such assumptions; but I also must honestly admit that a little boy still lives within me, a boy who saw raw, masculine power make things happen.

How can these conflicts be resolved?

As a Bahá'í, I believe that Bahá'u'lláh, as part of His mission to unite us, came to restore unity to the human spirit. His vision of that spirit draws back into one coherent whole those elements which we have projected into the world as dichotomies and embodied in conflicting values and institutions. Masculine and feminine, faith and reason, heart and soul, good and evil—these are but attributes of one reality.

"O Children of Men!" declares Bahá'u'lláh, *"Know ye not why We created you all from the same dust? That no one should exalt himself over the other. Ponder at all times in your hearts how ye were created. Since We have created you all from one substance it is incumbent on you to be even as one soul, to walk with the same feet, eat with the same mouth and dwell in the same land, that from your inmost being, by your deeds and actions, the signs of oneness and the essence of detachment may be made manifest."*

At another point, Bahá'u'lláh describes the central experience of His inner life, His Revelation, as a Maid of Heaven who proclaims His station to the world.

With this perspective, men can accept the feminine within themselves, knowing that differences between men and women have not been ignored, only transcended. When we accept that we are human beings first, that we are essentially one soul, we can draw on all differences—cultural and psychological—to reveal a unique, interesting man or woman.

I realize that I started to become a man, not when I wore my first jockstrap, or when I earned my degree, or when I married and became a father, or when I received my first credit card. I started when, confronting my own despair on a river boat in Vietnam, I realized that I could be free of fear only when I cared more about serving my buddies than about my own survival.

One afternoon I noticed the thick brush on both sides of a nameless river in South Vietnam. Suddenly I felt totally powerless. At any moment a sniper could shoot me or a grenade could explode the entire vessel, and I knew that nothing could prevent this. And I couldn't swim. At first, I waited to be killed, straining my muscles in anticipation, pleading for God's intervention through prayer. Exhausted, I stopped asking for God's guarantee when I accepted that there were no remedies for this specific situation in the prayers of Bahá'u'lláh.

O God, I thought, my life is in your hands. I will accept what will be. At that moment fear became pointless: For the time remaining I had a job to do and I could not do it by cowering in a corner. I got up and helped a guy who needed some salt pills. A few days later, while administering some medicine, I realized that I was happy. I had discovered a better self. I was a servant.

Traditionally, society has created rites of passage through which we affirm our identities. But sometimes experience presents us with the opportunity to face ourselves, to become more conscious of the possibilities latent within us. I now understand that manhood is not a status achieved through initiation rites. It is a process by which we face ourselves, ask the troubling questions, and seek the difficult answers. The great men, the heroes, are those who step beyond the confines of social and personal limit to pursue what the Plains Indians call a "vision quest"; and having found the object of their search, they return to give their gift to us, the gift of self-knowledge. But the road to self-knowledge is long, pot-holed, and swampy, a circular path with confusing signs. It is easy to get lost; we retreat as much as we advance. We are forced to go back and take another look, hoping that this time understanding will finally come.

It doesn't. There are too many contradictions, too many ironies for that one grand comforting conclusion. A life is not an essay.

And yet if we persist, going back again and again to examine those events which seem essential to our development, we can learn patience and tolerance on a long and winding road. It takes time to see what is around us. The guide who may lead us out of the forest just might be the one whose clothes we detest, whose lifestyle we abhor, whose values we disdain. A wise man accepts help from whatever source. I hope to deserve that title some day.

In the meantime, now as a school principal, I try to comfort those who are attacked on the playground for their inadequacy or physical incompetence, saddened by the knowledge that an old battle is still being waged. I resist the desire to leave my office to thrash the boys who attack the masculinity of others so glibly, and so make up for unhealed wounds and unfinished business.

I want to go to my father and say, "Dad, you hurt me. I love you." But somehow, I can't yet. I fear that in some way he will let me know once more that I have not measured up, that I am not man enough to suffer and love in silence. As I watch his body wither as cancer eats his lungs, I know that I cannot wait forever to face this fear—a fear unmatched even by the terror of jungle nights. But I am hopeful; recently he spoke to me about his childhood for the very first time, and I recognized that he had his own hurts. In his way, he was trying to reach out to me, and I think that soon we will acknowledge our brotherhood. We are both afraid of rejection. We are all afraid.

Sons and War Toys

by Melinda Armstrong

> *The way a child wants to play is often very different from the way his parents want him to. The child however, knows best.* —Bruno Bettleheim

"YOU PRETEND THAT YOU ARE IN THE TANK, and a missile flies over you and fires its weapons and you blow-up!" said the brown-haired boy crouched on the floor.

"I'm going to conquer the world," his brother screamed with his eyes squinted tightly and the corners of his mouth curled down. The metal objects crash, get thrown across the room, and the boys jump for joy.

"Awesome! A massive collision!" they cry out together.

"Let's do it again. This time I want to be the enemy!"

Their mother walks past the bedroom, which for today has become a battlefield and glances at the large, blue poster with white letters that reads: "*O God, guide me, protect me, illumine the lamp of my heart and make me a brilliant star.*"[1] Her body tenses as she listens to their dialogue, the anxiety of having her children growing up with these aggressive and violent behaviors distresses her, and she remembers the countless hours spent discussing peace with her once young and innocent boys. From her previous experiences, she knows it is useless to intervene; the more she protests, the more involved the play becomes.

Three rallies later, the boys shed their armor and run down the stairs, tripping over untied shoe laces and over each other's feet, in pursuit of their well-earned snack. Only seconds from the kitchen, they roll with laughter onto the floor locked in a wrestling hold. The enemy attacks the defender and the war games continue, only this rally is played with their bodies instead of their toys. The next sound heard is the piercing scream of the wounded—the youngest brother is crying out in pain for the care and protection of their mother.

Over the years, I have listened to women across the United States who are committed to working for world peace express their conflict over their sons' delight in war toys. A survey was conducted at Green Acre Bahá'í School in July 1986, and at the San Francisco International Peace Conference that same summer. That 75 parents responded to questions asking for their feelings and observations of their children's war play indicates that this subject is worthy of consideration. This essay will discuss how women respond to war toys in their children's play and what the implications are for the mother-son relationship.[2]

When women were asked how they felt when their children used power and aggression in their play, common responses were "anxious," "worried," "awful," "fearful of their character development," "needing to rechannel the play." Although many women recognize the natural tendency toward aggression in fantasy, they nevertheless felt conflicting emotions because of their desire that their sons demonstrate peaceful behaviors and attitudes. A few women expressed their disappointment and embarrassment with their sons' aggressive play.

In contrast to the strong reactions of women, a number of men expressed the need for a clarification of the question asked, as if it weren't completely understood. These men's answers were prefaced with lead-in questions such as: "Do you mean when . . . " or "Are you referring to when . . . " Most men responded with statements such as: "You must mean when the good guys defeat the bad guys. I have no feelings about this. I played with guns and arrows when I was a child and I turned out peaceful," or "I don't worry about this kind of play as long as no one gets hurt." Many fathers viewed the play as a necessary ingredient in learning life skills. Some men expressed concern and worry about aggression in their children's play, especially when it influenced the children's relationships with others.

Both mothers and fathers of daughters were less anxious, less concerned. Typical statements included the parents' understanding of their daughters' need to test limits and develop problem-solving skills, but with the anticipation that the behavior would be outgrown. The age of the child was a factor. Some women were more tolerant of aggressive behavior in younger children, and many women agreed that the aggressive behavior of their older children created feelings of aggression within themselves. In general, women responded with statements describing how the aggressive behavior in their children's play made them feel; whereas men tended to describe the behaviors specifically and find that aggressive play was acceptable, while aggression in actual relationships was not.

As for means to eliminate the aggressive behaviors in children's play, one woman wrote that if she could minimize television viewing, the violence would end. Another woman reported removing her son's toy guns from the house while he was sleeping. Yet another told of how she found herself yelling and screaming, while moralizing about the need for peace in the world and how her children should talk gently to one another.

Fathers' reactions were no less interesting. One father joined an organization entitled The National Coalition Against Television Violence, whose aim is to protest war cartoons which are specifically funded by toy companies to promote sales of their toys. Another father told of how he tried to substitute his son's need to wield a weapon in his hand with the concept of "turning swords into plowshares" by teaching him to pretend to be cutting tall grass with a machete. The trick worked successfully when the child played alone, the father reported, but when friends were over, the stick transformed back into a gun. Many fathers made references to the culture and the times their children are living in: "Our children are engulfed by a 'me-first' attitude which justifies aggressive actions between individuals, and by extension between nations. Until humankind evolves toward the understanding that we are one organic unit, our children will continue to see contradictions." Concluded one father: "If little boys model activities of their fathers, then when my son takes a hammer and nails to make something, that's natural. But when he takes his airplane and pretends to bomb whatever is below him, I too wonder about that need for power. But still, I don't worry about it too much. That's what little boys do."

The question of war toys is certainly not a new one. Children from all cultures adapt various objects from nature as toys to represent some form of hunting or fighting, although the level of aggression varies. Anthropological and sociological studies confirm a direct correlation between the level of aggression within the society itself and the attitude presented by children in their play.[3] Bruno Bettleheim in a paper on the importance of play states: "Children of the Middle Ages surely played at being knights and infidels, just as our own children play at being cops and robbers. Elizabeth I is said to have inquired whether the boys were now playing the war of the English against the Scots. In Europe early in this century, much play involved the Foreign Legion against the Arabs. And as soon as the wall went up separating West from East Berlin, German children began shooting at each other across miniature walls."

Ashley Montagu, in his studies of nonliterate societies,

writes in his book *Learning Non-Aggression*: "There are few societies in which some form of aggressive behavior, however slight, does not occur. The range of variation is striking, all the way from the wholly unaggressive Tasaday to the highly violent societies of the civilized world. The variability and absence of stereotypy suggest that violent behavior is largely learned. How else can one account for the marked differences in the expression of violence [in children's play]."[4]

The source of aggression and violence in human behavior has been a fascinating and controversial subject of research by developmental theorists, psychologists, and sociologists. Psychotherapist Alice Miller, in her recent ground-breaking study into the origin of violence *For Your Own Good*, renames the European concept of a "good upbringing," the "poisonous pedagogy." She believes the high term "child rearing" was misused by so-called educators and notables in the late 1700s and early 1800s. They called for the parents to use "mild corporal admonitions," to "become the master of the child forever," to "verbally chastise the child," and to "consciously humiliate to put an end to the child's innocence."[5] Willfulness, defiance, and obstinacy were dangerous faults that hinder the child's entire education and encourage undesirable qualities, according to J. Sulzer in "An Essay on the Education and Instruction of Children." He maintained that these behavior patterns should be driven out of the child by means of scolding and beating, and by not "giving in to their anger and tears."[6] Traditional notions of child rearing speak of the necessity of striking and humiliating children and robbing them of their dignity, while using such high-sounding words as "upbringing" and "guiding the child onto the right path."

The significance of Miller's work can be clearly understood when we examine our own sources of aggression. She believes that parents will manifest to their own children the hidden anger they accumulated from their childhood years in response to their own feelings of abuse and powerlessness. Here, tragically, the "poisonous pedagogy" repeats itself, as the unexpressed anger is transformed with time into more or less conscious hatred, directed against either the self or a substitute person. This hatred is released in various ways permissible and suitable for an adult. Miller concludes that not only is the individual child affected by this continued hidden power struggle, but also that we can all become future victims of this mistreatment.[7]

Margaret Mead in *Sex and Temperament in Three Primitive Societies* confirms: "The child who received a great deal of attention, whose every need was promptly met, as among the New Guinea Mountain Arapesh, became a gentle, cooperative, unaggressive adult. On the other hand, the child who received perfunctory, intermittent attention, as among the New Guinea Mundugomor, became a selfish, uncooperative, aggressive adult.

The challenge of learning from these studies and applying them to the education of our children is staggering. Humanity has from the beginning of time chosen aggressive means to resolve conflict. We now have the capacity to adopt a new way of thinking. From the Universal House of Justice's statement to the peoples of the world on peace comes the insight: "The entrenchment of the view that aggression and conflict are intrinsic to human nature and, therefore, ineradicable has paralyzed efforts to erect a system giving free play to individual creativity but based on cooperation."[8] Ashley Montagu confirms this need for change. He states that: "Whatever humanity's potentials for aggression may be, and we know that such potentialities exist, it is clear that their expression will largely depend upon the environmental stimulation they receive. If this is so, then there is every reason for optimism, for if we understand the conditions that produce aggressive behavior, there is some hope that by changing those conditions we may be able to control both its development and expression."[9]

Why, then, are families that are working to change their consciousness toward world peace by changing aggressive and violent behavior in their children's play experiencing difficulty and conflict? Implicit in the responses from parents about their attitudes toward aggression in their children's play is the fact that the conflict seems to lie within the parents, not within the children. Apparently, the battle of war toys is being fought by parents. Little boys are certainly enjoying their play, while therapeutically fulfilling their need for empowerment and working out the conflict of good against evil. Further, the interviews indicate that the conflict is experienced primarily by women, who are noticing a detrimental side effect to their reactions to their sons' aggressive play. These women find that the more they resist with moralizing and lecturing, the further their sons seem to reject their own more feminine qualities and relate more to masculine images perpetuated through our culture and projected by the media. The problem is doubly great for Bahá'í women, who are striving to feminize their families by upholding the principle of the equality of men and women and to transform the war-like qualities of man into peace-loving qualities. (Parenthetically, the men interviewed were not threatened by the distancing of their sons that the women felt.)

Families interviewed believed that, despite their efforts to spend quality time with their children, they are continually challenged by outside influences such as television, peer-pressure, today's morality, and their own personal histories. One woman wrote: "I felt very close to my sons when they were younger—praying, consulting—basically, being sensitive. I find, now that they are older, it seems as though they relate all those spiritual activities as "female activities," while trying so hard to create their own identity. I am repelling them from me when I react to their war games, or even to the aggression they express, through words. They are beginning to reject everything associated with femininity. I look back at all those wonderful times we spent together when they were babies and ask: Have they bonded to their culture more than to our spiritual values?

In his report, "The New Family," Harvard graduate student and Bahá'í, Rhett Diessner states: "Nancy Chodorow has investigated the psychological interaction between mother and daughter, mother and son, (and lack thereof between father and children) that I believe have implications for the difficulties found in the identity process for both sexes. Mothers have a perpetuated mutual relationship with daughters that is comprised of primary identification and dependence. Whereas with sons, from the age of infancy, the mother-son relationship tends to emphasize independence and individuation. However, as boys tend not to interact with their fathers (as fathers are "away at work"), they tend to define their identity as much not-female as pro-male. Boys come to view (inter)dependence and attachment as not-male; girls due to lack of independence and separation suffer from an inability to define an autonomous self stemming from an overwhelming sense of responsibility for, and in connection to, others. Chodorow's solution is for boys to have fathers who take a major role in childrearing; and recommends girls to have mothers who have a valued role and recognized sphere of legitimate control."[10]

We are living in an age of imbalance and unwholeness. The voice of one-half of the world's population is yet unheard. Half of humanity has been excluded from public decision-making and action. Psychological theories of human and moral development are being challenged, theories by which reality has been defined for the past hundred years. Carol Gilligan, in her book *In a Different Voice*, maintains that woman's voice must be established as equal but different.[11] Her research indicates that the approaches of men and women differ when making moral decisions. According to her, "men and women may perceive danger in different social situations and construe danger in different ways—men seeing danger more often in close personal affiliation than in achievement and construing danger to arise from intimacy, women perceiving danger in impersonal achievement situations and construing danger to result from competitive success." Is it any wonder that women find war toys threatening to the connectedness of the family unit?

If in fact *"woman [is] by nature opposed to war; she is an advocate of peace,"* and *"A mother who has tenderly reared a son for twenty years to the age of maturity, surely she will not consent to having that son torn asunder and killed in the field of battle."*[12] Why would she not be threatened even by the play at aggression and violence she sees in younger sons? War toys and aggressive play become a metaphor for woman's lack of "power and privilege" in attaining a right of vote and control in human government. *"Woman is naturally the most devoted and staunch advocate of international peace."*[13]

If sons and war toys can be seen as a metaphor for women and peace, then the interviews suggest the need for a positive response to boys experimenting with aggression and war games, rather than the current hostile reaction to it. If peace education is taught in another context, if the need for the elimination of all forms of prejudice is demonstrated in every part of life, and if the principles of equality are at work within our families, parents need not fear that their sons will manifest later in life the aggressive behaviors of their play.

Boys can be taught positive feelings toward masculinity and femininity. Both boys and girls can learn justice with intuition, and rational thought with sensitivity. They can learn to blend, in a single act, these complementary ways of dealing with the world. Boys can cry and laugh, play war and talk about peace. The aggression in the children's play as demonstrated through their war toys will not be a threat to their future development, for they will have developed the tools of caring balanced with a sense of justice. War toys will no longer be valued as the forbidden fruit.

As we attempt to paint a complete picture of moral development and sexual equality, a subject just beginning to have the rough edges sketched in, the following vignettes illustrate the dynamics at work in families contemplating the role of war toys in children's play.[14]

Phyllis's Story. "The only way I can start talking about Tobey's involvement in war play, is to explore a little history on my husband's side of the family.

"Jon's mother raised four boys, essentially on her own. She was a product of her times, and she had a husband with a military career who was away for long periods of time. For the most part, she discouraged war toys, and forbade things which depicted war, such as television shows, 'Combat' and 'Rat Patrol,' etc.

"Even as a peace-promoting adult, Jon admits that he has sought out the very things she tried to keep him away from. He shows great interest in war history in all its particulars. With time and observation, I have come to believe that it is the tactical and strategic aspects of these goings-on which hold such fascination for him, the elements of human intelligence and cooperation which go into making conventional warfare. He has also been moved deeply by the compassion which wartime evokes in people, prompting them to show the best parts of themselves for the benefit of others.

"Aside from being a promoter of the ego, war is, I'd venture to say, an amazing expression of the human soul's two greatest capabilities. Those who planned for warfare have demonstrated impressively sophisticated forms of complex thinking and planning. Indeed, the very complexity of what they wrought could so absorb them, that it served to distance them from the unspeakable horror of what they were planning. Those who have carried out the plans of their leaders, have often demonstrated the epitome of human love in the sacrifices which they make for others. Knowing and loving have always been there, but seldom in balance.

Thus, the extremes of knowledge without compassion, and loyal (loving) obedience without wisdom, have combined to perpetuate an institution now potentially fatal to all.

"Where does Tobey's war play fit in? I speculate that as he gropes to establish his place in this world, the tools of war are those of personal empowerment with which to carry out the budding seeds of analytical thinking within himself. If his sense of personal power is strong, then his other abilities will have value in his eyes, and he will work to express them.

"He has really been struggling to feel secure in life recently, particularly in school. The other day he was involved in a word exercise there, matching single syllable words with the picture tiles they named. Afterwards, his teacher asked him to select four of the tiles, write the names of the objects pictured, and illustrate them. One of the tiles showed a revolver. He chose it first, and executed a freehand drawing which was remarkably sophisticated in accuracy and detail, far in advance of his age level. He literally poured everything he had into making that drawing. His other illustrations were accurate, but the barest renderings of the objects selected. The teacher reinforced his effort with strong encouragement, recognizing that it had been a powerful point of personal assertion and expression for him. He has since been devoting similar effort to other art work.

"I have begun questioning the role each parent plays in dealing with war-related behavior in boys. It has become clear to me that I defeat my purpose in the negative ways in which I respond to Tobey's activity of this sort. I am mouthing platitudes and incomplete ideas which only serve to widen a gap between us. I am not finding the positive seeds of development within his expression and reinforcing them, as the teacher did. I am not respecting and valuing his efforts to express different ways of thinking, and bringing those to the forefront of his awareness.

"Jon's response to this behavior, on the other hand,

might be to introduce the tempering influence of compassion which women typically demonstrate: 'Now that you have captured them, and you're the king, how can you make your kingdom a nice place to live in?'; or maybe even asking him how he *feels* when he's wielding a Construx sword or a Lego lazer gun.

"If we reinforce knowing and loving in these complimentary ways, I hope that he can feel good enough about himself, and feel enough unconditional acceptance from us, to be open to the other kinds of education. Then we can share our ideas about the inability of war to resolve problems, and the importance of being a knowing and loving part of the cooperative alternative."

Pat's Story.

WAR TOYS

> Mommy, I want a gun.
> *But guns kill.*
> Mommy, I want a machine gun.
> *You could get hurt.*
> Mommy, see *that* gun?
> That's the one I want!
>
> Gee Mom, everyone's got a gun.
> They're fun!
> It's only a toy.
> It's not *REAL.*
>
> *No, it's not real.*
> *REAL guns kill*
> *and REAL guns are bad*
>
> But mommy, *I'm* not bad.
> *I* just want to play.

To play
To play
To play . . .

   To play war.
No, to play power.
   To play death.
No, to play control
   To play destruction.
No, protection.
So the "bad guys" won't get us.
   Oh . . .

"The bad guys were the preoccupation of my young sons' activities. They made forts and traps and acquired various weapons of defense, all to get the bad guys. Sometimes they took turns being the bad guys. But mostly the bad guys were other groups of kids in the neighborhood.

"I wanted everybody to get along, to be friends, but that wasn't the way it was. And my children were not the peace-makers I wanted them to be. They had a black-and-white way of viewing the world. You were either good or bad, for me or against me. There were no shades of gray. This simplified view of the world was easier for them to deal with.

"If I'd been a single parent, I probably would have tried to prohibit the boys from playing with war toys, but my husband introduced them into the home. Projectile toys, darts, squirt guns, BB guns, arrows, sling shots, and other various and sundry items of destruction. My attitude only changed when they wisely encouraged me to participate. They *were* fun. They required great skill and gave immediate results.

"And upon reflection, my own childhood was just the same. There were the good guys and the bad guys, the winners and losers. And as an adult, I'm now capable of recognizing good and bad, godly and ungodly, positive and negative. What has evolved is an adult understanding of people. That people are not all good or bad. That each person contains a dual nature.

"Still I was concerned about the effect that playing with these toys or games would have. They seem to encourage a desire for power, *singular* power—to be the 'king of the mountain.' I was concerned about my children's desire to overpower other human beings, to inflict harm upon them, to control someone else, and the false glory which surrounds these toys and games.

"So I compromised. I did not spend my money on them. They would not receive them from me on their birthdays. But I would not prohibit them from owning or playing with them. It was my husband's responsibility to teach the boys safety standards. We both tried to teach the boys what the toys were really about.

"I did notice that the more helpless the boys felt, the greater their interest in power. Lessons not learned in school resulted in war games in the afternoon. Their interests were a barometer to their inner condition. This is just one of the gauges that parents can use to determine what's going on in their child's life, or to assess the type of person he or she is becoming.

"The toys and games we choose to play are only symptoms of inner yearnings. Yearnings for power, or desire to be a winner. That today we have an explosion of aggressive war toys on the market, and that our boys are fiercely attracted to them, seems only appropriate considering the times. That they want to be winners and have control over their environment is good. What we need to remember is that these toys and games are only outward expressions of inner desires, that our children's loves and hates, desires and ambitions, are shaped by us, not them."

Implicit in Phyllis's and Patty's stories, and in the words of women interviewed, is the mother's desire for sons who would play peacefully and nonaggressively. These women expressed varying degrees of disappointment and anger when their expectations were not met. Many of these women came to recognize within themselves an unconscious negative attitude towards masculinity. This the result of living in a male-dominated culture. But they found that their capacity to respond creatively to their sons' war play was thereby immobilized.

Linda Schierse Leonard speaks to this occurrence in her book *The Wounded Woman, Healing the Father-Daughter Relationship*. In it she says, "The father is the first experience a woman has of the masculine. In this way, he provides an important model for the way she relates to man and to her own inner masculine side." Many women suffer from a poor self-image, from the inability to form lasting relationships with men (including sons), or from a lack of confidence in their ability to work and function in the world. These women may appear to be successful business-women, contented housewives, or carefree students. But underneath lie wounded women, damaged by "a bad relation to their personal father, or wounded by the patriarchal society which itself functions like a poor father." Her solution lies in healing the father-daughter wound and in culturally restructuring the balance of power. The call once again is for woman to rediscover the feminine. Only then can a positive vision of femininity be returned to the man and son. According to Leonard, this essential step is paramount in the making of peaceful men.

Even while they are quite young, mothers must come to terms with the masculine strivings of their sons. And while masculinity—as femininity—has many dimensions, one of the most basic involves the opposing roles of hero and outlaw, good guy and bad guy. Boys will inevitably play at power and aggression and be fascinated by the conflict of good and evil. Mothers who find that they have few positive images of masculinity to call upon, perhaps because of their own childhood experiences, will find themselves disturbed and frightened by this. They will be unable to encourage the heroic and positive elements in these childhood games. Their negative reactions will not stop the war play, as the experiences of all of the women interviewed clearly demonstrate, but they will erect barriers between mother and son.

War, after all, is an adult problem, not a child's problem. Can a five-year-old boy really understand the tragedy of fighting and killing, or the destructive power of an atomic bomb? As boys play at their war games, they can only mimic the images and behaviors of the world that surrounds them. And this in a constant effort to define their own identities amidst the confused signals our society gives them. The complexities of world peace, the subtle moral arguments for nonviolent behavior, are beyond their grasp. They must first define themselves in positive ways before they can approach the world and its problems.

And so, perhaps the question of war toys is a misplaced one. Surely it is a mistake for any adult to make a child feel bad about himself for wanting to act out in fantasy the roles of power and aggression that he sees around him, and which will eventually be integrated into his own masculine identity. As we have seen, such an approach is counterproductive.

Whether or not a child will play with war toys is not a central issue. Whether or not he will build a positive identity and maintain strong relationships within the family is a very central one. The mother who sacrifices the quality of her relationship with a son in exchange for an absence of war toys in his room has made a poor choice. Their mother/son relationship must be able to withstand the twists and turns that the crafty toys cannot. It must last from one birthday to another, and from one holiday to the next. It should not be threatened by the next plastic pistol that emerges from the gift wrapping.

Such a relationship, however, requires that women come to positive terms with masculinity, as well as with their own femininity. The challenge is to create the delicate balance in both men and women that humanity needs and longs for.

Notes

1. A prayer for children revealed by 'Abdu'l-Bahá. *Bahá'í Prayers* (Bahá'í Publishing Trust: Wilmette, Ill., 1954) p. 15.

2. Neither the expertise of the author nor the scope of this article will allow for a serious treatment of the father-son relationship with regard to issues of empowerment, competition, sex role formation, and Oedipal development.

3. Ashley Montagu, ed. *Learning Non-Aggression: The Experience of Non-Literate Societies* (Oxford University Press, 1978) p. 6.

4. Ibid., p. 5. The Tasaday of Mindanao live in the Philipines. Until 1966, the Tasaday were an exclusively food-gathering people. It is interesting to note that although "classic" aggressive behaviors among toddlers were observed, adults retained no such patterns. Anthropologists suggest that the Tasaday reward cooperative behavior and discourage aggressive conduct, while creating positive models for their children to imitate.

5. Alice Miller, *For Your Own Good: Hidden Cruelty in Child-rearing and the Roots of Violence* (New York: Farrar, Straus, Giroux, 1983).

6. Ibid.

7. Ibid., p. 262.

8. From the statement of the Universal House of Justice, "The Promise of World Peace," 1986.

9. Montagu, *Learning Non-Aggression*, Introduction.

10. Nancy Chodorow, "Family Structure and Feminine Personality" in M. Rosaldo and L. Lamphere, eds., *Women, Culture and Society* (Stanford, Calif.: Stanford University Press, 1974) p. 43–67.

11. Carol Gilligan, *In a Different Voice: Psychological Theory*

and Women (Cambridge, Mass.: Harvard University Press, 1982) p. 42.

12. 'Abdu'l-Bahá, *The Promulgation of Universal Peace* Howard MacNutt, comp., Revised Edition (Wilmette, Ill.: Bahá'í Publishing Trust, 1982) p. 375.

13. Ibid.

14. Phyllis's story was kindly contributed by Phyllis Ring. Pat's story was authored by Patricia French. I am grateful to both contributors for their help.

Biographical Notes

MELINDA ARMSTRONG lives in southern New Hampshire with her husband and three sons. She taught first grade for seven years prior to founding and becoming editor of *The Spiritual Mothering Journal*.

R. JACKSON ARMSTRONG-INGRAM, Ph.D., received his doctorate from the Queen's University of Belfast, Northern Ireland. His dissertation traces the history of music, devotions, and aesthetics in the North American Bahá'í community. He is currently continuing research on other areas of Bahá'í history.

ESTHER BRADLEY is a writer living in the Los Angeles area. She is currently at work on a biography, but is considering the publication of a handbook, "The Womanly Art of Refrigerator Cleaning."

PEGGY CATON, Ph.D., received her doctorate in ethnomusicology from the University of California, Los Angeles. She has conducted research on Persian music in Iran and is currently Music Editor for *Encyclopaedia Iranica*, Director of Research for the Institute of Persian Performing Arts, and is an independent consultant in intercultural relations.

GLORIA HAITHMAN, Ph.D., is Director of the Norman Topping Student Aid Fund Office at the University of Southern California and is an active member of the Black

Staff and Faculty Caucus. She received her doctorate in Urban Studies from that institution and lectures in the field of public administration.

KATHRYN JASPAR taught as an associate professor of English for twenty years. She is now a free-lance writer and painter living in St. Peters, Missouri. She is an active member of the Planning Committee for the Women's Alliance of the Greater St. Louis area.

BAHARIEH R. MA'ANI, currently a member of the Bahá'í World Centre staff in Haifa, Israel, is a descendent of the early Nayriz Bábís. She studied philosophy and religion at Pahlavi University in Iran and at the University of Nairobi in Kenya.

JUDY MADDOX is a free-lance writer and mother of four in Lynnwood, Washington. She is Director of Media Management, a marketing research firm, and owner of Northern Light Productions, which produces audiovisual materials for Bahá'ís.

SIDNEY MORRISON is a Middle School Principal in Torrance, California, and an editor for *dialogue* magazine. He studied history and education at the University of California, Los Angeles. He is married and has three children.

MUHTADIA RICE is a Los Angeles-based entrepreneur. As a feminist, she has appeared on national talk shows to discuss women's issues. She and her daughter reside in Southern California and on the Kona Coast of Hawaii.